ARE YOU DECEIVED?

What your Ministries, Teachers,
Priests, Reverends and Government
do not want you to know and
will not tell you!!!

By
George Zerubbabel

Note for Librarians: A cataloguing record for this book is available from Library and Archives Canada at www.collectionscanada.ca/amicus/index-e.html
ISBN 1-4120-5312-9

Printed in Victoria, BC, Canada. Printed on paper with minimum 30% recycled fibre. Trafford's print shop runs on "green energy" from solar, wind and other environmentally-friendly power sources.

TRAFFORD

Offices in Canada, USA, Ireland and UK
This book was published *on-demand* in cooperation with Trafford Publishing. On-demand publishing is a unique process and service of making a book available for retail sale to the public taking advantage of on-demand manufacturing and Internet marketing. On-demand publishing includes promotions, retail sales, manufacturing, order fulfilment, accounting and collecting royalties on behalf of the author.

Book sales for North America and international:
Trafford Publishing, 6E–2333 Government St.,
Victoria, BC v8t 4p4 CANADA
phone 250 383 6864 (toll-free 1 888 232 4444)
fax 250 383 6804; email to orders@trafford.com
Book sales in Europe:
Trafford Publishing (UK) Ltd., Enterprise House, Wistaston Road Business Centre,
Wistaston Road, Crewe, Cheshire CW2 7RP UNITED KINGDOM
phone 01270 251 396 (local rate 0845 230 9601)
facsimile 01270 254 983; orders.uk@trafford.com
Order online at:
trafford.com/05-0207

10 9 8 7 6 5 4 3 2 1

Table of Contents:

1

6.666 What it really means. Is it a real mark on/in your forehead or in your right hand? God also has a seal that goes in your forehead. Which seal or mark do you have? Pgs. 72-95

7.Speaking in tongues, as in babble, (like Babylon which means confusion) is not in the Bible. You do not have to speak in babble tongues to be saved. This is not true and directly against God's word. Pgs. 96-101

8.Rapture, as in fly away is a lie and not in the Bible. It is a tradition of men to give false security rather than the truth of God's word. Pgs.102-115

9.Easter is not in the manuscripts. It is a pagan tradition of Fertility worship and sexual orgies.
Quick like a rabbit.Pgs.116-126

10.God is a divorcee. Pgs.127-128

11.There is no such thing as reincarnation. Pgs. 129-133

12.Are the sins of the Fathers carried through the third and fourth generation? NO! this is not true and has a qualifier for this saying which many leave out. Pgs. 134-136

Introduction

Are you deceived?
This is a really dumb question by definition. If you are deceived you couldn't possibly know that you are. The definition of deceived says that you believe something to be true even though is may be false; however, you are blinded by the facts you believe to be true. Not because they are true, only because the source you believed was not genuine and true but smooth and felt good.

By the time you have read this book you will learn that many of the things you have been taught as true are not really true. They are the twisted and embellished teachings of man. Sort of like the pass it on thing we did as children. Put ten people in a circle, tell the first person a fact and each whisper this to the next person and have the last person tell you what he heard. Wow, nothing like the original. So here we begin unraveling the story back to the original truth.

We have History as a witness, the Bible as a witness and prophesy, past, present and future as a third witness.

By reading this book you will learn that: There are three Earth and three Heaven ages. We are in the second Earth and Heaven age. Why we are here and what the purpose of us being here is. This is evidenced by the calamity that destroyed the dinosaurs in the first Earth and Heaven age.

We will learn the truth as to who, why and how this was accomplished.

There was no apple in the Garden of Eden. Satan deceived Eve and then Adam into believing his doctrine rather than the words of God. Satan convinced them that if they listened to him and disbelieved God that they would become like gods themselves, knowing better than God. Satan seduced Eve and she later had two sons, one by Adam and one by Satan, Cain and Abel. This is why they covered their genitals with fig leaves as they were ashamed of what they had done when God showed up.

All of the Ethnic tribes were created on the 6th day and God said they were very good. Each tribe has their own special talent, kings and ways of doing things. All of these tribes make up the whole of God's children.

There is no such thing as reincarnation. We were all here in the first Earth and Heaven age in our spirit bodies. This is why they have never found bones; however, they have found foot prints in Archeology dating back to the dinosaurs.

We will learn that there really arc UFO's. They have been identified and we call them IFO's (identified flying objects). We will learn about the good angels and the evil fallen angels, why and how they fell and where they are now. And we will learn about the offspring of the fallen ones called Emims or Giants.

5

We will learn the truth about this 666 everyone seems concerned about and the mark associated with this.

We will learn that America is written about in the migrations of the scattered tribes of Israel. How the tribes came to America and why this all happened. We will also look at the future prophesies concerning Samaria, Ephraim and Manassah, I mean America.

We will document that Easter is a carry over from Pagan traditions carried over from our captivity in Babylon and has no place in the House of God. It is an abomination and refers to worshiping the goddess of fertility and orgies. We will see how this came to be.

We will learn that speaking in tongues is also a perversion of what happened on Penticost day. Man has taken the true speaking of the Holy Spirit through the Apostles and claims in his own mind that he is speaking (babbling) some mysterious secret language that no one knows except God. If we bring these perversions to the Touch Stone of truth we see that they are comical and we begin to ask ourselves, how silly man is in his imaginations when he strays from the truth?

The rapture theory that is being taught is extremely dangerous as it will cause the deceived to follow the Antichrist, False Christ, Satan and his fallen angels. If we bring this to the true Rock or touchstone and not the false rock we will see the true gold.

Once we see and hear the TRUTH we can only sing the song of

> (Revelations 15:3) And they sing the song of Moses the servant of God, and the song of the Lamb, saying, Great and marvelous are Thy works, Lord God Almighty; just and true are Thy ways, Thou king of saints.

It is easy to understand that when building a house all parts must fit together; straight, plumb, level, true and must have a solid foundation, otherwise the house cannot stand. Let us take the House of God and His children for example.
There are 12 signs in the Zodiac
There are 12 tribes to Israel.
The Zodiac forms a circle in the Heavens.
The 12 tribes were camped in a circle under the heavens.
The four major tribes were camped at the 4 cardinal compass points; N, E, S, and West.
The earth rotates in a circle so that we have 12 hours of day and 12 hours of night or 2X12 hours in a day as we call it.
The earth rotates so as to give us 12 months in the year.

7

The Priests were to wear a breastplate with 12 stones in it representing the 12 tribes of Israel.
There were 12 Patriarchs.
There were 12 Apostles.

In the center of the encampment of the tribes of Israel was the Temple of God.

It now looks like God took a compass, stuck in the point and drew a circle around His creation and then gave specific directions through Moses (the Law) as to how His children are to pitch their tents for protection against their enemies. There were Giants in the land in those days and there was the progeny of Satan also who had mingled with the Nephilim or Fallen Angels that produced the Giants.

Doesn't it also stand to reason that God would also give further directions to His children as to how to operate in this life in order to stand against the enemy? Yes! We have one who was supposed to protect the Truth and God's children in the Age that was. He fell and wanted to take over God's position and has fought against God, HIS children and God's Angels since his fall. We will document all of this.

Let's take an example of man following foolish ideas. Trying to build his own salvation like, going along with building the tower of Babel because they believe not the truth and are seduced, beguiled, deceived, or are looking for a fast way to God without following His directions.

8

(Genesis 11: 3-9.3 And they said one to another, Goto, let us make **brick**, and burn them thoroughly. And they had brick for stone, and slime had they for mortar.4 And they said one to another, Go to, let us build us a city and a **tower, whose top may reach unto heaven**; and **let us make us a name, lest we be scattered abroad upon the face of the earth**. 5. And the LORD came down to see the city and the tower, which the children of men builded. 6. And the LORD said, Behold, the people is one, and they have all one language; and this they Begin to do: and now nothing will be restrained from them, which they have **imagined** to do.

God takes action lest men would figure out how to live forever in their evil, unrighteous flesh.

7. Go to, let Us go down, and there confound their language, that they may not understand one another's speech. 8. So the LORD scattered them abroad from thence upon the face of all the earth: and they left off to build the city. 9. Therefore is the name of it called Babel; because the LORD did there confound the language of all the earth: and from thence did the LORD scatter them abroad upon the face of all the earth.

Strong's Concordance tells us that:

9

Brick: is translated from (H-3835) To be or become <u>white</u> from (H3443) from the whiteness of the <u>clay (altar of) brick</u>, tile.

Imagined: (H-2161) a prime root; to plan, <u>usually in a bad sense:-consider, devise, imagine, plot, purpose, (evil)</u>.

Babel: (H-894) from 1101; confusion to <u>mingle, mix, confound</u>.

Rightly divided; The people were of one language and decided to **build a white brick tower, altar** reaching into heaven where God sits and **make their own name, like Jim Jones ministry,** or they **would be scattered by the enemy.**

First mistake: They wanted, by their own hands, to build a white brick altar that reached into Heaven without God.

Second mistake: They wanted their own name, not God's name.

Third mistake: they would be scattered if they didn't build this tower when truth is, they would be scattered **IF** they built it.

Who told them this anyway? You'll soon see.

Here is what Jesus says about this.

(John 10: 1+10): Verily, Verily, I say unto you, He that entereth not by the door into the sheepfold, <u>but climbeth up some other way, the same is a thief and a robber.</u>(10) <u>The thief cometh not, but for to steal and to kill and to destroy;</u> I am come that they might have life and that they might have it more abundantly.

Now we "see" that we have the thief and robber who wants to destroy and kill AND we have the one who came to bring life in abundance. GOOD=THE LORD BAD= THE ENEMY

Now we know that the one instigating or suggesting the building of their own religion, altar and name was really the enemy; Satan the destroyer and his children, the offspring of Cain.

2 Corinthians: 13-15 For such are false apostles, deceitful workers, transforming themselves into apostles of Christ. (14) And no marvel; for Satan himself is transformed (disguised) as an angel of light. (15) <u>Therefore it is no great thing if his ministers also be transformed (G 3345 disguised) as the ministers of righteousness;</u> whose end shall be according to their works.

Here we are today and this is what our LORD has to say about the goings on this day through Ezekiel.

(Ezekiel 13: 10) Because, even
because they have seduced My people
saying, Peace; and there was no
peace; and one built up a wall, and
lo, others daubed (plastered) it
with untempered mortar.

Untempered: (H-8602) From an unused root
mean to smear, plaster (as gummy) or
slime; (fig) frivolity:-foolish things,
unsavory, untempered.

This same Tower of Babylon appears in
other places throughout God's word; as
the Asherash white pillar of grove
worship and ending with Babylon
(confusion) of;

> (Revelations 17:5) And upon her
> head was a name written Babylon
> **(confusion)** the great, the mother
> of harlots and abominations of the
> earth.

Companion Bible identifies Harlots of
the Earth.

**Babylon is the fountain-head of all
idolatry and systems of false worship.**
This is the "mystery of iniquity" (2
Thes, 2, 7) seen in all the great
"religions" of the world. All alike
substitute another god for the God of
the Bible; a **god made with the hands** or
with the imagination, but equally made;
a religion consisting of human merit and
endeavour.

Now we begin to see how subtle and cunning Satan, Lucifer, the one who appears as an angel of light really is and it is so important to rightly divide God's word or Satan will lead you up the wrong tower or into the wrong flight out of here or have you chasing eggs and bunny rabbits while forsaking the true high holy day of Christianity and gobbling like a turkey.

Our state of degradation has come so far and we have come so low that we actually have to have a lizard tell us what insurance to buy or a dog to tell us what fast food we should eat. Lets now move on to answering some important deceptions taught by the ones disguised as ministers of righteousness.

Chapter I

America in the Bible

Is this America The Beautiful today?

Are you living under; Debt, fear, confusion, depression, stress, poverty and disease? **It is written**, America, the past and the future. The TRUTH will set you free from lies and bondage.

We are going to show that the Kenites (sons of Cain) would have us believe that we are Heathen and that they are the chosen ones when in reality, we are the chosen ones and they are liars. When we loose our knowledge, history and roots we may then be taken into slavery at their command. Well, we're on our way there.

This is why the schools, colleges and churches do not want to teach the TRUTH about Jacob's pillar (stone of Scone) which has been carried by the tribes throughout history and sat for many years under the coronation chair of the Kings and Queens of England. Their pledge was "keepers of the faith". They are so scared that America may really learn their roots and return to the Living God of Israel and He should take pity on us and rip up our enemies and His enemies. This is going to happen one way or another. We can either learn and be blessed or remain ignorant and perish for lack of knowledge.

Let us move on now to learn the HISTORY about our roots.

The truth is: America is written of in the Bible.

Traditions of men, stories about miracles that happened to old Uncle Charlie or Aunt Emma are nice but they don't tell you what His-Story has to say, rather they lead you away from the power of righteousness and truth. They make void the truth by their traditions and you become unarmed, without a shepherd or the wrong shepherd and ripe for slaughter by the wolves, spiritually and physically, or should we say wolves dressed in sheep's clothing.

America the Beautiful

This goes way back into Biblical History when the Father of Many Nations **(Abraham) believed God** and walked with our Father in TRUTH, RIGHTEOUSNESS and FAITH. These are some of the promises God made to Abraham and his <u>seed or offspring</u>, mainly some of us.

From; "Abrahamic Covenant" by E. Raymond Capt. (Pg.2). Abraham was promised a tremendous number of descendants. God later changed the name of Jacob to Israel. (Gen.35:10) so his inheritors who were the inheritors of the covenant were hereafter known as Israel. Jacob had 12 sons, each the head of his own family. These families developed into the 12-tribed nation of Israel (Gen. 35:22). Jacob, hereafter called Israel,

15

loved Joseph more than all his other
children, (Gen. 37:3) and before Israel
died, Joseph brought his two sons to his
father to be blessed. Israel (Jacob)
crossed his hands and laying his hands
on their heads, blessed the sons of
Joseph – Ephraim and Manasseh. He then
said, " And let my name be named upon
them." "Thus his adoption of the two
sons of Joseph created another tribe
making thirteen tribes in all. Israel
refused to uncross his hands, so
Ephraim, was set before Manasseh (Gen.
48: 16-20). Thus Manasseh became the
thirteenth tribe and received the
promise of becoming a great nation.
Ephraim was given the promise of
becoming a company of nations (i.e. v
48)."

Let's read on and "see" that Manasseh
(which means forgetful) is the United
States of America, "One Nation under
God" and that 13 is the basis of our
National Ensign (Heritage i.e. Flag). We
are the thirteenth son or tribe as we
will soon learn.

From: (Pg.34 of Abrahamic Covenant by E.
Raymond Capt.) "In like manner much could
be shown by history and tradition that
the United States of America is from the
tribe of Manassah and is peopled by a
gathering of all thirteen tribes of
Israel. Our Pilgrim fathers, who called
themselves, 'the seed of Abraham God's
servant and the children of Jacob, His
chosen,' allotted their land as Israel
did. They followed after the council of
Moses, the lawgiver of Israel and in all
their undertakings, asked for guidance and

blessings from the God of Jacob, Isaac and Abraham.

From Manassah, the thirteen tribes of Israel has come our national number, thirteen. Our first colonies were thirteen in number. There are thirteen letters in our national emblem, the 'American Eagle' (Job 39: 27-30; Deut. 28:49;Psalms 103: 5; Exodus 19:4). The Eagle holds in it's right talon an olive branch with thirteen leaves (Jer. 11:16; Psalms 128:3; Gen. 49:22) and in it's left, thirteen arrows plainly illustrating God's command given to the Israelites (Deut.20: 10-12). In it's beak the Eagle holds the scroll on which is written, in thirteen letters, 'E Pluribus Unum,' (One out of many) and above this is a cloud in which shine thirteen stars (Luke 2: 9; Num. 9: 17;10: 34; Psalms 105: 39; Exodus 13: 21; 14: 19-20;16: 10; 24: 16; 34: 5; 40: 38). There are thirteen bars on our flag and thirteen rods in our National mace. On the reverse side of our Great Seal is shown a symbolic pyramid. It's suspended apex stone portrays the all seeing eye of the Almighty, watching over the destiny of our nation. The pyramid identified with the Great Pyramid of Giza (Isaih19: 19-20), consists of thirteen letters'Annuit Coeptis' (He has favored our beginnings). Altogether, there are thirteen '13's' in our heraldry. Our flag is made up of the colors scarlet, blue and white, the colors of Israel of old. These colors covered the table of shew bread within the tabernacle. Red is the color of blood and signifies justice or judgment,

reminding us of the shed blood of Christ
for the redemption of His people Israel;
White, signifying purity or holiness,
the color of snow; (psalms 50: 7; Isaiah
1: 18). Blue the color of the sky
signifying love and because this is the
color of the heavens it is
representative of God.
The name Manasseh means 'forgetfulness'
and if there has ever been a people
forgetful of all their past, it is this
last , this thirteenth, this Manasseh-
Israel people in the United States.
However, America, as prophesied of
Manasseh, did become a great nation, One
out of many, (E Pluribus Unum) and took
her place in the appointed time, in
fulfillment of God's covenant with
Abraham."

Our Dollar bill has the all seeing eye
of God at the top of the pyramid and the
stone that the builders rejected has not
returned to take His place as the Head
Stone.

Are you beginning to see where the Lost
Tribes of Israel were scattered to?

For further history of the migrations of
the tribes after the Babylonian
captivity, through Europe, Ireland,
Scotland and over the Caucus Mountains
to the Americas and further
clarification and study of this rich
heritage we have, order the book;
"Abrahamic Covenant, by E. Raymond
Capt." Through King's Chapel or
Shepherd's Chapel at the end of this
book.

Here is what God has to say about, all
the tribes including, the 13th tribe,
Manasseh, one out of many, of the so
called lost tribes of Israel.

(Isa.44:21) Remember these, O
Jacob and Israel; for thou art
my servant: I have formed thee;
thou art my servant: O Israel,
thee shalt not be forgotten of
Me.

Do not forget the LORD!

(Deut 8:10-14) Lest when thou
hast eaten and art full, and
hast built goodly houses, and
dwelt therein; And when thy
herds and thy flocks multiply,
and thy silver and gold is
multiplied, and all thou has is
multiplied; Then thine heart be
lifted up, **and you forget the
LORD thy GOD**, which brought thee
fourth out of the land of Egypt,
from the house of bondage;
(Deut 18: 43) the stranger that
is within thee shall get up
above thee very high; and thou
shalt come down very low. 44 He
shall lend to thee, and thou
shalt not lend to him; he shall
be the head, and thou shalt be
the tail.

Here we are in America the Beautiful.
Under the heavy bondage of debt and the
tax man. Our wealth and our heritage is
being trashed and we have become
debtors. We work for lower wages than
we were paid 30 years ago.

We have children killing children,
unsafe streets and unrighteous judges,
ruling against our Constitution, with
total disregard for the people.

WARNING!!!
If you really would like a picture of
America today read the rest of the
cursings in (Deut.18:43).

(Rev.2: 5) <u>Remember therefore
from whence thou art fallen, and
repent</u>, and do the first works,
or else I will come unto thee
quickly and remove thy
candlestick out of its place,
except thou repent.

It is time to hold our Teachers,
Reverends, Preachers, Judges and Leaders
accountable for truth, righteous
judgments and protection of our valuable
heritage.

(Eze.34: 2) Son of man,
Prophesy (preach)<u> against the
shepherds</u> of Israel, prophesy
(preach), and say unto them.
Thus saith the Lord God unto
the shepherds; **woe** <u>be to the
shepherds of Israel that do
feed themselves!</u> Should not the
shepherds feed the flocks?

This is to you who sit in the Churches
(Bethavens)= empty houses called by
God's name.

Heb 5:12 For when for the time
ye ought to be teachers, ye
have need that one teach you
again which be the first
principles of the oracles of
God; and are become such as
have need of milk, and not of
strong meat.

This means that you are ignorant
of God's words and truth, shame on
you, you should know enough to be
teaching and instead all you know
is repentance and salvation. This
is good but it is only milk, baby
boomers.

Woe: Strongs (H-1945) from 162, a prime
word expressing pain exclamatory; Oh! -
ah, alas. From 188, owy,o-ee; prob. From
183; (in the sense of crying out after);
lamentation.

**You Shepherds who are in it for the
money,** you better take heed---WOE to
you!!!

2 Tim 4:3-4 For the time will
come when they will not endure
sound doctrine; but after their
own lusts shall they heap to
themselves teachers, having
itching ears; 4 And they shall
turn away their ears from the
truth, and shall be turned unto
fables.

We must learn the difference between the Holy and the Profane, between righteousness and unrighteousness, between clean and unclean lest we perish.

Our forefathers knew these things when they set up our Constitution under GOD where our laws originated from Exodus, Leviticus and Deut.

Do we really want what is left of our heritage taken from us?

> Matt 7:14-15 Because strait is the gate, and narrow is the way, which leadeth unto life, and few there be that find it.
> 15 Beware of false prophets, which come to you in sheep's clothing, but inwardly they are ravening wolves.

In order to do this we must rightly divide truth from lies and traditions of men and hold the unjust accountable. It is not a light thing.

Jesus is Telling us; (1 Jn. 2: 5) (**if you love me you'll keep my words**) Look back at the Laws of Moses, the school master, and learn the rules of Fathers house so that we may please Him.

Jesus also knows that none of us could do all the laws as in legalistic.

That is why He came among us, Emanuel (God with us) " The Word was made flesh and dwelt among us" (Jn: 1: 14) and brought us forgiveness through repentance by His blood and He is faithful to forgive. So, today while it is today, all we have to do is to repent (have a change of mind) ask forgiveness and try to do righteousness, justice and truth.

This means keeping HIS words not man's words.

> John 3:16-18 For God so loved the world, that he gave his only begotten Son, that whosoever believeth in him should not perish, but have everlasting life.
> **17 For God sent not his Son into the world to condemn the world; but that the world through him might be saved.**

So don't listen to those wolves who tell you to do this tradition or that tradition or you will go to hell. It is a lie. If the LORD doesn't condemn you who do they think they are that they are greater than God? Oh! we forgot, Satan and HIS ministers are the accusers (Rev:12 10). Get the picture?

> John 3 18 He that believeth on him is not condemned: but he that believeth not is condemned already, because he hath not believed in the name of the only begotten Son of God.

23

Look in the BOOK for therein we find
what is good, what is right, and the
keys to the way the truth and the life
filled with blessings and not cursings.

**John 8:32 And ye shall know the
truth, and the truth shall make
you free.**

John 14:6 Jesus saith unto him,
I am the way, the truth, and the
life: no man cometh unto the
Father, but by me. **2 John 3:
Grace be with you, mercy, and
peace, from God the Father, and
from the Lord Jesus Christ, the
Son of the Father, in truth and
love.**

Chapter II

No apple spoken of in the Garden of Eden !

Let us begin at the beginning in the book of Genesis

The name "Genesis" is not even a Hebrew word, but a Greek rendition out of the Septuagint, which is part of the Torah. The original Hebrew name of this book was "The Beginnings".

The word "apple" is not to be found anywhere in the Book of Genesis, but is contained throughout the literature used in Bible study groups, usually for children.

> (Gen.2: 9) And out of the ground made the LORD God to grow every tree that is pleasant to the sight, and good for food; **the tree of life** also in the midst of the garden, and the **tree of knowledge of good and evil.**

Life: (H-2416 from 2421) chayah, khaw-yaw; p prime root to live, whether lit. of fig,; caus. To revive- keep (leave,make) alive, x certainly give (promise) life, (let, suffer to) live, nourish up, preserve (alive) quicken, recover, repair, restore (to life), revive, surely be whole.

We have two trees; the tree of life representing Christ/God and the tree of good and evil representing Satan the deceiver.

After Jesus healed the blind man, this is what the healed man, whose eyes were opened to the TRUTH said. Mark 8:24 And he looked up, and said, **I see men as trees**, walking. After Jesus opened his blind eyes.

Man has a choice; life or death and guess what? Man makes the wrong choice.

> (Ecc.1: 9) The thing that hath been, it is that which shall be; and that which is done is that which shall be done: and there is no new thing under the sun.

The same choice in the end will be coming again, when Satan stands in the Holy Place claiming to be Christ/God, (tree of life) when he is actually the tree of death as God said. Don't eat of this tree and Satan's false doctrine or you will surely die (Gen. 2: 17).

Christ's first warning!!

> (Matt. 13: 5) And Jesus answering them began to say, <u>Take heed lest any man deceive</u> you:

26

Matt:(6) For many shall
come in my name saying, I
am Christ; and shall
deceive many.

Calling themselves Christians
and Christian preachers,
ministers and teachers.

Genesis:2[16] And the LORD
God commanded the man,
saying, Of every tree of
the garden thou mayest
freely eat: [17] But of
the tree of the knowledge
of good and evil, thou
shalt not eat of it: for
in the day that thou
eatest thereof thou shalt
surely die.

Let's look up the word used for TREE
in the Hebrew section of Strong's
Concordance.

Tree: (H-6086) atsah, aw-tsawb; a
prime root; prop. To fasten (or make
firm), i.e. to close (the eyes):-
shut.

Moving along to Adam and Eve:
Gen:2[25] And they were both
naked, the man and his wife,
and were not ashamed.
Genesis 3:1 Now the serpent
was more subtil than any beast
of the field which the LORD
God had made. And he said unto
the woman, Yea, hath God said,
Ye shall not eat of every tree
of the garden?

27

Serpent: (H-5175) from (5172) naw-khash; a prime root; prop. To hiss, i.e. whisper a (magic) spell; gen. To prognosticate:-x certainly, divine, enchanter, (use) x enchantment, learn by experience, x-in-deed, diligently observe.

Subtil: (H-6175) aruwm, aw-room; past part of (6191) a prime root; prop. To be (or make) bare; but used only in derog. Sense (through the idea of smoothness) to be cunning (usually in a bad sense); take crafty counsel, be prudent, deal subtly.

Did you ever see a serpent talk?

Satan is about to; enchant, whisper as in hypnotize Eve while twisting God's Word. He was MIS-quoting God as he also did when he tried to tempt Christ in the wilderness with God's own Words albeit with a spin on it.. (takes lots of --- to use God's words on God Himself). It is satins MO, his greatest method of deception. By misquoting, adding too, deleting and twisting the scriptures and causing people to believe his version of what is written, instead of the "truth" of what is really spoken by God.

> Gen 3:[2] And the woman said unto the serpent, We may eat of the fruit of the trees of the garden:

Eve knew that she and Adam could freely eat of all the trees of the garden except one (the tree of

knowledge of good and evil). Repeating
what God commanded.

> [3] But of the fruit of the
> tree which is in the midst
> of the garden, God hath
> said, Ye shall not eat of
> it, neither shall ye touch
> it, lest ye die.

Touch: (H-5060) Naga, naw-gah; a
prime root; prop,to touch, i.e. lay
the hand upon (for any
purpose;euphem, to lie with a woman);
by impl. To reach (fig. To arrive,
acquire); violently, to strike
(punish, defeat, destroy, etc.).

Satan has now brought into question
the Word of God. Eve, in her reply,
omits the word "freely" (before, 'eat
thereof'), adds the words "neither
shall ye touch it", and alters the
certainty "thou shalt surely die" into
a contingency "lest ye die". She is
wavering at God's word and hasn't
even been listening to the Serpent's
twisted scripture one full day.

> Gen 3: [4] And the serpent
> said unto the woman, Ye
> shall not surely die:

Satan now reverses the Word of God and
tells the first of many, many lies,
for he is the father of lies (John
8:44).

If the tree of the knowledge of good
and evil, which is in the midst of the
garden, is Satan, what is the fruit

spoken of here?

It is real simple. Fruit is that which is "produced" by a tree. Here is what Christ said:

> Luke 6:43-44 For a good tree bringeth **not** forth corrupt fruit; neither doth a corrupt tree bring forth good fruit. [44] For every tree is known by his own fruit...

> Genesis 3:4 And the serpent said unto the woman, Ye shall not surely die: [5] For God doth know that in the day ye eat thereof, then your eyes shall be opened, and ye shall be as gods, knowing good and evil.

It is their "spiritual eyes that will be closed as in the prime Hebrew of the word TREE.! We are not talking about eating apples.

Their flesh eyes are opened to good and evil and they realize that what they did was not holy and righteous and was directly against God's commandment. What then? They, WE cover it up.

We are all born with that small little voice (spirit) within us that tells us what is right and wrong. As we grow older we fall away and IF we realize what that voice was, our first love, though now scar tissue, we are invited to repent and return through His grace and blood, Christ is faithful to forgive , heal us and welcome us home.

You aren't alone. It happens to all of us.

> [6] And when the woman saw that the tree was good **for food,** and that it was **pleasant to the eyes,** and a tree **to be desired** to **make one wise,** she took of the fruit thereof, and did eat, and gave also unto her husband with her; and he did eat.

Satan sure has a way of convincing us that if it; tastes good, feels good, looks good and will make us wise we go for it.

Hey Alice! Give me another beer? If you get the idea.

There has been a touching going on as defined by Strongs. To lie with a woman.

> [7] And the **eyes of them both were opened, and they knew that they were naked;** and they sewed fig leaves together, and made themselves aprons.

Now they are wiser, yes, and they aren't covering their mouths with fig leaves. They now know that they are in big trouble with God and that they are ashamed and naked before Him.

> [8] And they heard the
> voice of the LORD God
> walking in the garden in
> the cool of the day: and
> Adam and his wife hid
> themselves from the
> presence of the LORD God
> amongst the trees of the
> garden.

Let's see what kind of fruit this orgy
in the Garden produced?

> (Genesis 4: 1-2) And Adam
> knew (had intercourse with)
> Eve his wife; and she
> conceived, and (9 months
> later) bare Cain, (not a
> baby apple) and said, I have
> gotten a man from the LORD.
> (2) And she **again** (as in
> continued in labor) bare
> his brother Abel.
> And Abel was a keeper of the
> sheep, but Cain was a tiller
> of the ground.

Again: (H-3254) yacaph, yaw-saf; a
prime root; to add to augment (often
adv. To continue to do a thing).

Did you notice that Eve had one son
and then kept on in labor and had the
other son. Yes, as in fraternal twins
by two different fathers.

You all know the story about Cain and
Abel. Well, guess which father
produced the son (fruit) who Murdered
his own brother?

32

The fruit from the bad, death tree
that God told Adam and Eve to stay
away from.

Satan had beguiled Eve, he totally,
wholly seduced her. That is why the
apostle Paul would say in his second
letter to the Corinthians, that he had
espoused them (the church) to one
husband, and he wanted to present them
as chaste virgins to Christ. But he
was fearful that they would become
"spiritually" seduced, even as Eve was
"physically" seduced by the serpent.

You see, Eve was a chaste virgin
before Satan seduced her.

> 2 Cor.11:2-3 or I am
> jealous over you with godly
> jealousy: for I have
> espoused you to one
> husband, that I may present
> you as a chaste virgin to
> Christ.

The subject is presenting a chaste
virgin to be Christ's wife at the
marriage of the Lamb.

[3] But I fear, lest by any
means, as the serpent
beguiled (wholly seduced)
Eve through his subtilty, so
your minds should be
corrupted from the
simplicity that is in
Christ.

Beguile: (H-5377) naw-shaw; a prime
root; to lead astray, i.e. (ment.) to
delude, or (mor.) to seduce:-beguile,
deceive, X-greatly, X-utterly. (G-
1818) expatao, ex-ap-ap-ah-o; from
1537 and 538; **to seduce wholly:** -
beguile, deceive.

Eve lost her virginity in the flesh as
an example of how deception in our
minds can cause us to loose our soul
to the false one's deceptions,
traditions and lies.

Chapter III

Three Earth Ages

We are going to show and document that there are three Earth ages and three Heaven ages.

That in the first Heaven and Earth age Satan drew a third of God's children into following him.

That God wiped out, completely destroyed the first Earth age because He was loosing His children to Satan's tricks, false teachings and deceptions.

What's new under the sun? Satan is operating with the same MO here again.

That God took His children back with Him into our spirit bodies and decreed that all would go through the flesh bodies having free will, being innocent of what happened in the first Earth age so that all His children would be on equal ground, having the same free will chance to see the true workings of Satan and possibly will abhor what they see going on and turn to the Father and his righteousness after seeing Father's wonderful works of salvation by Yeshua and love for His children.

That God then created the Earth and Heaven age we are in now.

That God is going to destroy this Earth and Heaven age and bring us all into the millenium and third Earth and Heaven age where Satan will be bound (unable to influence us) and Father's truth and righteousness will rain down upon all who were blinded, beguiled and led astray.

That at the end of the third Earth and Heaven age (Millenium) would come the Great White Throne Judgment, Satan would be releases for a short while and those whom he is able to deceive as well as those who hate God will be blotted out forever along with Satan.

Let us begin by opening one of Jesus' dark sayings and bring it into light.

This has a two fold meaning. One must be born into the flesh through the water breaking and then die in the flesh in order to enter heaven in our Spirit Man with the LORD and secondly one must also die to the things of this world (as symbolized by Baptism. The going into the water and regenerating anew into life) and love the LORD more than the promises of Satan.

> John 12:24-25 Verily, verily, I say unto you, Except a corn of wheat fall into the ground and die, it abideth alone: but if it die, it bringeth forth much fruit.
> 25 He that loveth his life shall lose it; and he that hateth his life in this world shall keep it unto life eternal.

This is the root of the fallen angels
who left their place of habitation,
without falling into the ground as in
being born of woman.
And those who followed Satan and his
false teachings in the first earth age
as well as those who follow him in
this earth age. The command is to love
things of the earth less than you love
the LORD.

Now the beginnings.

(2 Peter 3:5-7) For this they
willingly are ignorant of, that by
the Word of God the heavens were of
old, and the earth standing out of
the water and in the water: Whereby
the **world that then was,** being
overflowed with water**, perished**

Let us correctly translate the Hebrew
using Strongs Exhaustive Greek, Hebrew
dictionary and get to the real meaning
of what happened and why we are here
in the flesh.

The Earth and the heavens were of old
and perished.

Was: (H-1961) Strongs; hayah, haw-yah;
a prime root/ to exist, i.e. be or
become.

So in the beginning, way back when, the
earth became void (empty) and without
form.

How did it get that way and why?

We will learn about that earth age soon.

Perished: (G-622) Strongs; apollumi, ap-ol-loo-mee; from 575 and the base of 3639; to destroy fully (refl. To perish, or lose) lit. or fig..--destroy, die, lose, mar, perish.

The Earth and Heaven age that then was, perished, was destroyed, died, finished.

(Genesis: 1: 1-3) In the beginning God created the heaven and the earth. And the earth **was** (became) without form, and void; and darkness was upon the face of the deep. And the Spirit of God moved upon the face of the waters.

(Jer. 4: 23-26) I beheld the earth, and, lo, it was **without form, and void; and the heavens, and they had no light.**

(24) I beheld the mountains, and, lo, they trembled, and all the hills moved lightly.
(25) I beheld, and, lo, **there was no man, and all the birds of the heavens were fled**. No ! not even Noah ! No birds either.
(26) I beheld, and, lo, the fruitful place was a wilderness, and **all the cities thereof were broken down** at the presence of the LORD, and by his fierce anger.

OH! There really was an Atlantis.

Our Father, the Creator shook this old planet (probably using natural phenomenon) and knocked it off of its true axis and out of its original orbit.
That is why there's a magnetic variation between magnetic north and true north.. The earth now "wobbles on it's axis" which causes the jet streams, fierce winds and storms.

In the world that then was, the first earth age, there were dinosaurs (Job: 40-15) that we know about and have witnessed, frozen solid in the Arctic regions with buttercups still in their mouths. All habitations, cities like Atlantis. Etc. were wiped out. Geologists prove that there was a severe cataclysm.

The destruction was so complete that even the heavens had no light, which is why God, in the creation of the second Earth and Heaven age (this one), commanded "let there be light". Now there was light in the days of Noah, but not after the destruction of the first Earth and Heaven age.

There was no man and all the birds of heaven were fled. This couldn't have been Noah's flood.

There were survivors and birds. Trees survived like the olive branch Noah's dove brought back after the waters receded.

You should now begin to see that we were here in our spiritual bodies

during the first earth and heaven age
when our Father became so angry with
Satan and one third of His children
that he overthrew the world that then
was. We all were taken home as Father
made a decree that He would create a
new earth and heaven.

> (Rev 12:3-4) And there appeared
> another wonder in heaven; and
> behold a great red dragon, having
> seven heads and ten horns, and
> seven crowns upon his heads. (4)
> And his tail drew the third part
> of the stars of heaven, and did
> cast them to the earth;

Because of the rebellion of Satan, as
we just read in Revelation 12, he drew
one third of the sons (stars) of God
away from Him and deceived God's
children into following him (Satan).
Ezekiel 28, tells us about, Satan, the
false rock and Tyrus.

Here is what Satan really looks like.
No pitch fork or horns here!!!!

> (Ezekiel 28:12-19) Son of man,
> take up a lamentation upon the
> king of Tyrus, and say unto him,
> Thus saith
> the Lord GOD; Thou sealest up the
> sum, full of wisdom, and perfect
> in beauty. (13) Thou hast been in
> Eden the garden of God; every
> precious stone was thy covering,
> the sardius, topaz, and the
> diamond, the beryl, the onyx, and
> the jasper, the sapphire, the
> emerald, and the carbuncle, and

gold: the workmanship of thy tabrets and of thy pipes was prepared in thee in the day that thou wast created. [14] Thou art the anointed cherub that covereth; and I have set thee so: thou wast upon the holy mountain of God; thou hast walked up and down in the midst of the stones of fire.(15) Thou wast perfect in thy ways from the day that thou wast created, till iniquity was found in thee. (16) By the multitude of thy merchandise they have filled the midst of thee with violence, and thou hast sinned: therefore I will cast thee as profane out of the mountain of God: and I will destroy thee, O covering cherub, from the midst of the stones of fire. (17) Thine heart was lifted up because of thy beauty, thou hast corrupted thy wisdom by reason of thy brightness: I will cast thee to the ground, I will lay thee before kings, that they may behold thee. (18) Thou hast defiled thy sanctuaries by the multitude of thine iniquities, by the iniquity of thy traffick; therefore will I bring forth a fire from the midst of thee, it shall devour thee, and I will bring thee to ashes upon the earth in the sight of all them that behold thee.

The stones that covered Satan were the stones worn in the breast plate of the priests representing the twelve tribes of Israel (Ex. 39: 8-14). Satan's favorite place is the pulpit.

WARNING!! Check out everything your are told against God's word.

Satan has been judged to be cast as profane out of the mountain of God. God said He will destroy him after he is cast to the earth and he, Satan will be laid before kings as he is burned into ashes from within and it shall devour him in the sight of all them that behold thee.

Now lets go to this Earth age where we have LIGHT and DARKNESS. Light is Christ, the word of God and darkness is Satan, the false Christ or Antichrists (instead of Christ). God says that we are children of light (like the sun) and Satan is darkness (like the moon). See! The moon has no light of it's own. It is a reflection of the true light of the sun.

> (Genesis 1:3) And God said, Let there be light: and there was light. (4) And God saw the light, that it was good: and **God divided the light** from the darkness
> (John 8:12) Then spake Jesus again unto them, saying, **I am the light** of the world: he that followeth me shall not walk in darkness, but shall have the light of life.

Even in the beginning of this Earth age, God divided; light from darkness, Cain from Able, Tree of Life and Tree of knowledge of good and evil, day and night.

We can clearly see the things created as a parallel to things of heaven.

Example: We must come through the water of the womb to enter into this life in the flesh. We must be baptized through the water to enter into life with Christ in our spirit men.

Look around at all the parallels between Heaven and Earth in this Earth age and you begin to see the wonderful works of the LORD, and the terrible works of Satan.

When we see the parallels like: Every thought you have comes from somewhere? Right? It begins within your Spirit or it begins in your Flesh. Feed me Etc. If your Spirit is righteous then your thoughts will be also and the fruit you produce will be good. If your thoughts are evil or bad then your fruit will also be evil or bad. Fact of life. It is like the computer phrase we use, "GARBAGE IN GARBAGE OUT", BIG PROBLEM IN AMERICA AND MUCH OF THE WORLD TODAY !!! If we are not taught the difference between that which is right and good the flesh takes over and we have nothing to govern ourselves by or with. We end up watching the fruit of this with Rapes, Murders, Children killing children or their parents and we also have parents murdering their babies. This is not a mental illness. It is our fault for not adhering to and teaching that

which is right and just and pleasing
to the LORD of the Universe. He sets
the laws of Gravity, seasons, as well
as what is righteous, clean and
unclean. If you look around at the way
Satan's workers have twisted the
truth, made wrong right, the unclean
as though it were clean and they have
taught traditions of man instead of
God's truth. This has made God's words
of righteousness of none effect. Look
around and open your eyes and you will
begin to abhor Satan's works of
unrighteousness, ungodliness,
uncleanness and his hate for God's
children. We do not want this to
continue.

(2 Peter 3:13) Nevertheless we,
according to his promise, look
for new heavens and a new earth,
wherein dwelleth righteousness

Remember Jesus' first warning.

(Mark 13: 5-6) And Jesus
answering them began to say,
Take heed lest any man deceive
you;(6) For many shall come in
My name saying, I am; Christ;
and shall deceive many.

I am is Father's sacred name, so they
will be saying that they are Christ's
(Christian) representatives, ministers
of righteousness. Don't be
deceived!!!!

(2 Cor. 11: 13-15) For such are
false apostles (preachers),
deceitful workers, transforming

44

(disguising) themselves into apostles of Christ. (14) And no marvel; for satan himself is transformed (disguised) into an angel of light. (15) Therefore it is no great thing if his ministers also be transformed (disguised) as ministers of righteousness; whose end shall be according to their works.

Now we are ending this Earth age; **666** ; after Satan has been cast to the earth in the sight of men, standing in the holy place calling himself Jesus and God. This is the 6th trump, the 6th seal and the 6th vial of Revelations. Note: the true Christ does not return until the 7th trump, 7th seal and 7th vial of Revelations.

We'll talk about this more in the other questions about 666 and the false rapture doctrine.

If you would like more in depth study please order books from Kings Chapel or Shepherd's Chapel as in Acknowledgements.

Chapter IV

All Ethnic Races were created on the 6th day, man and woman. Adam was formed on the 8th day. Why and what is the purpose of this?

Lets document some of this and then we will look into it to see what the purpose of all this is.

Gen 1:26-27 And **God said, Let us make man in our image**, after our likeness and let them have dominion over the fish of the sea, and over the fowl of the air, and over the cattle, and over all the earth, and over every creeping thing that creepeth upon the earth.
27 **So God created man in his own image, in the image of God created he him; male and female created he them**.
Gen 1:28 **And God blessed them, and God said unto them, Be fruitful, and multiply**, and replenish the earth, and subdue it: and have dominion over the fish of the sea, and over the fowl of the air, and over every living thing that moveth upon the earth.
Gen 1:31 And **God saw every thing that he had made, and, behold, it was very good. And the evening and the morning were the sixth day.** KJV

The Hebrew translation of man is: OT:120 **'adam (aw-dawm')**; from OT:119; ruddy i.e. a human being (an individual or the species, **mankind, etc.): all of the races.**

Did you notice that God; created us all
in our exact image(Phantom) as God and
the angels (which is what we are when we
are not in our flesh bodies), blessed
them and said they were very good.

Image in Hebrew: OT:6754 tselem (tseh'-
lem); from an unused root meaning to
shade; **a phantom**, i.e. (figuratively)
illusion, **resemblance**;

Moving on to the 8th day man Adam.

First, the reason why God created a
special type of man. The man Adam.

Hint: The entire bible and plan of God
involves a special unmixed genealogy
through which Christ would come to save
all of God's children from Satan who is
called death. The Bible documents
clearly how Satan has tried to stop,
interfere with and hinder God's plan
from the beginning.
This is part of the reason for the
bloody battles throughout the bible,
Satan in the Garden of Eden, the Flood
of Noah, Sodom and Gomorrah, Jonah and
the whale and Jericho, to indicate a
few.

All of the men God had created so far
were fishermen, hunters and Keepers of
the cattle and animals.

Then came the seventh day wherein God
rested and then on the eighth day we now
look in and see what is going on.

Now the eighth day.

Gen 2:5-8 And every plant of the field before it was in the earth, and every herb of the field before it grew: for the LORD God had not caused it to rain upon the earth, and **there was not a man to till the ground**. 6 But there went up a mist from the earth, and watered the whole face of the ground. 7 And the **LORD God formed man (Hebrew haa'aadaam: the man Adam) of the dust of the ground, and breathed into his nostrils the breath of life; and man became a living soul.** 8 And the LORD God planted a garden eastward in Eden; and there he put the man whom he had formed. KJV

"See", this man Adam in Hebrew is a specific man, a farmer to till and take care of the garden. You might say like a Husbandman. A keeper of the vineyard.

This specific genealogy through which Christ would come, the Lamb without blemish or spot to save God's children by HIS blood. This is the reason for all of the battles whereby Satan tries to mingle the perfect genealogy and prevent Christ from coming. Reason for Noah's flood, destruction of Sodom and Gomorrah and many other battles in the Bible.

Gen 2:15 And the LORD God took the man, and put him into the garden of Eden to dress it and to keep it. KJV

Adam was supposed **to Dress** the Garden: OT:5647`abad (aw-bad'); a primitive

48

root; to work (in any sense); And to Keep the Garden:OT:8104 shamar (shaw-mar'); a primitive root; properly, to hedge about (as with thorns), i.e. guard; generally, to protect, attend to,

Adam messed up right off the bat. He wasn't watching and protecting the Garden.

Right then and there Satan and Adam both impregnated Eve in the first orgy in the GROVE and she had fraternal twins, Cain by Satan and Abel by Adam. Then again Satan caused Cain to murder his brother Abel trying to prevent the seed line of Christ. Adam then had another son named Seth to carry on the genealogy to Christ (Gen: 4 25).

Adam fell short and began listening to the spin Satan put on God's words, "do not eat of Satan's false doctrine. It will kill you." But it looked and felt good. Yep! Nothing new under the Sun.

God created all of the Races for a reason. Each race has a special gift or talent. When all work together according to God's rules and the TRUTH we begin to see the wonderful creation and works of God and all things become possible.

Satan and his children do not want this so they use the oldest trick in the book. Divide and conquer. Weaken and enslave the minds first, then the flesh.

Chapter V

UFO'S in the Bible

We are going to document; that UFO's do exist.

God's throne was carried aboard a UFO or in our case identified flying object IFO.

Angels that visited the prophets were our brothers, not aliens, they are just like us.
There are evil angels or fallen angels (aliens if you wish) who left their place of habitation (heaven) and came to earth in defiance of God's command to go through the flesh in this earth age without any knowledge of the previous Age that was and they were destroyed. There have been more than one invasion of fallen angels who tried to interfere with God's plan of salvation by Christ and were destroyed.
There will be another influx of fallen angels who will come upon earth called a swarm of locusts because they will spiritually destroy with their false doctrines just like the physical Locusts eat up all green things.
Satan himself will be cast out of heaven to earth along with his angels. He will be claiming to be the tree of life like he did in the Garden of Eden when he is actually the tree of the Knowledge of Good and Evil (death) and if you touch him, listen to him, follow him, support him, you will die, spiritually because he is called death.

Let us begin with Ezekiel's description
of a UFO as he observed. Remember that
Ezekiel never saw anything other than an
Ox Cart or a Chariot.

Ezek 1:44 And I looked, and, behold,
a whirlwind came out of the north, a
great cloud, and a fire infolding
itself, and a brightness was about
it, and out of the midst thereof as
the colour of amber, out of the midst
of the fire. Ezek 1:16 The appearance
of the wheels and their work was like
unto the colour of a beryl: and they
four had one likeness: and their
appearance and their work was as it
were **a wheel in the middle of a
wheel**.

Gee, sort of like God told the tribes
to make their camp. Camp in a circle,
all 12 tribes with the Temple and Ark
of the Covenant in the middle of the
circle. A circle within a circle.

Alright men! Pull the wagons in a
circle.

Ezek 10:9-10 And when I looked,
behold the four wheels by the
cherubims, one wheel by one cherub,
and another wheel by another cherub:
and the appearance of the wheels was
as the colour of a beryl stone.
10 And as for their appearances,
**they four had one likeness, as if a
wheel had been in the midst of a
wheel**.

Ezek 10:11 When they went, they went
upon their four sides; they turned
not as they went, but to the place
whither the head looked they
followed it; they turned not as they
went.

Today we can visualize this like looking
at passengers that go where the airplane
goes.

Ezekiel is describing a UFO which
carried God's throne as well as the four
protecting gun ships so to speak.

We are His children and there is an
enemy who would like to take us captive
and use us as slaves in the flesh and
bring our spirits or souls into his
death camp. The only way we can stand
against this arch enemy of God and you
and me is to know the TRUTH.

Here Elijah is taken up by a UFO as
described by Elisha who witnessed it.

**2 Kings 2:11-12 And it came to pass,
as they still went on, and talked,
that, behold, there appeared a
chariot of fire, and horses of fire,
and parted them both asunder; and
Elijah went up by a whirlwind into
heaven.**
12 And Elisha saw it, and he cried,
<u>My father, my father, the chariot of
Israel, and the horsemen thereof.</u> And
he saw him no more: and he took hold
of his own clothes, and rent them in
two pieces.

Today we would have some nut case

running around saying the Elisha had been abducted by an Alien.

What did Elijah, who witnessed this say as he recognized God's vehicle?

"My Father, my father, the chariot of Israel". No different than you seeing Air force One and identifying it because of the flag and markings on the vehicle.

Do you know what the insignia is on God's vehicle? Universe One?

Hint: It is the same marking used to identify the 4 major tribes of Israel as they camped and it is the same markings on the zoon or as we would say Gun Ships who guard God's vehicle. OK. Here it is:

> Ezek 1:10-11 As for the likeness of their faces, they four had the **face of a man**, and the **face of a lion**, on the right side: and they four had the face of an **ox on the left** side; they four also had the **face of an eagle**.
> 11 Thus were their faces:…..

Also representing the encampment of the Tribes, E,N,S,W: Judah = Lion, Dan=Eagle, Reuben=Man and Ox=Ephraim

Think about this! God's throne was within the circle of the encamped 12 tribes. A circle within a circle.

Now let us look at Angels or Aliens, our brothers, that actually spoke with man.

Rev 22:8-9 And **I John saw these things**, and heard them. And **when I had heard and seen, I fell down to worship before the feet of the angel which shewed me these things.**
9 Then saith he unto me, **See thou do it not: for I am thy fellowservant, and of thy brethren the prophets, and of them which keep the sayings of this book**: worship God.

Here John is describing an angel of the LORD.
A supernatural being who has come from Heaven to deliver a message. This is also the same way that Satan's supernatural angels have come and will once again come to Earth with Satan when he is cast out of Heaven and arrives proclaiming that he is the Christ and God. He is the Antichrist, the False Prophet.

If we have the seal of God (God's Word TRUTH not mans traditions) in our foreheads and the gospel armour (Eph: 6: 11) on we shall be ready to stand against Satan.

God promised that He would protect us and give us power over all our enemies, IF!(Jn:14 23) we keep HIS words. This means we need to know the TRUTH of God's words not mans foolish traditions.

See, when we know the whole story we are

fully protected by God, the creator of the entire Universe. We are HIS children and HE loves us a great deal.

Here is what Jesus says to those who see the TRUTH, love the LORD and follow HIM.

Luke 10:17-19 And the seventy returned again with joy, saying, Lord, even the devils are subject unto us through thy name.18 And he said unto them, I beheld Satan as lightning fall from heaven.19 Behold, I give unto you power to tread on serpents and scorpions, and over all the power of the enemy: and nothing shall by any means hurt you.

Luke 10:20 Notwithstanding in this rejoice not, that the spirits are subject unto you; but rather rejoice, because your names are written in heaven. KJV

(Luke: 21: 18) But there shall not an hair of your head perish.

When we get the time line correct. This next verse does not happen until the end of the Millenium (1000 Yrs.) with the LORD and Satan is released for a short time to try and deceive God's children again.

Matt 25:41): Then shall he say also unto them on the left hand, Depart from me, ye cursed, into everlasting fire, prepared for the **devil and his angels:**

Two more of our Super Brothers, Angels or Messengers show up on the scene to tell Ezekiel what says the LORD to Israel (America and free Christian Nations = Israel= 10 Lost tribes).

Ezek 40:3-4 And he brought me thither, and, behold, **there was a man, whose appearance was like the appearance of brass**, with a line of flax in his hand, and a measuring reed; and he stood in the gate.4 And the man said unto me, Son of man, behold with thine eyes, and hear with thine ears, and set thine heart upon all that I shall shew thee; for to the intent that I might shew them unto thee art thou brought hither: declare all that thou seest to the house of Israel.

Two super natural men of God, Angels, coming into Sodom. Why are they going to destroy Sodomy? Because of the Nephilim or fallen angels and all the perverted wickedness that was going on. Check out the story. (Matthew: 24 37) They were eating and drinking and giving in marriage. To Who? The fallen Angels.

Gen 19:1-2 And **there came two angels to Sodom at even**; and Lot sat in the gate of Sodom: and Lot seeing them rose up to meet them; and he bowed himself with his face toward the ground; And he said, Behold now, my lords, turn in, I pray you, into your servant's house, and tarry all night, and wash your feet, and ye shall rise up early, and go on your ways. And they said, Nay; but we will abide in the street all night.

Gen 19:15 And **when the morning
arose, then the angels hastened Lot,**
saying, Arise, take thy wife, and
thy two daughters, which are here;
lest thou be consumed in the
iniquity of the city.

**Jacobs ladder reaching into Heaven where
he saw Angels.**

Gen 28:12 And he dreamed, and
behold a ladder set up on the
earth, and the top of it reached to
heaven: and behold the **angels of
God ascending and descending on it.**

The stone that Jacob laid his head on
when he had the vision or dream is
called the Stone of Scone and has been
under the coronation chair of the Kings
and Queens of England all these
Centuries and part of the ceremony is,
"Keeper of the Faith". For more
Information write to or call King's
Chapel or Shepherd's Chapel for the
booklet, Stone of Scone.

Now we will see that we have a celestial
or spirit body as well as a terrestrial
body or earthly dust body.

1 Cor 15:38-40 But God giveth it a
body as it hath pleased him, and to
every seed his own body. All flesh
is not the same flesh: but there is
one kind of flesh of men, another
flesh of beasts, another of fishes,
and another of birds.
There are also **celestial bodies, and**

57

bodies terrestrial: but the glory of the celestial is one, and the glory of the terrestrial is another.

Terrestrial is Earthly while Celestial is Heavenly.

We should also remember that Satan also has his angels called the fallen angels who left their place of habitation (heaven) and came to earth in violation of God's command to go through the flesh and they took daughters of Adam and had children known as the giants or Geber. This was the reason for the Flood of Noah, and the destruction of Sodom and Gomorra. Also, satan is the great imitator of Christ and of the Holy Ghost (Spirit). Do you know which spirit you are listening to?

God talking to Job. Morning stars and sons of God mean, all of us here and our spirit men.

Job 38:6-7 Whereupon are the foundations thereof fastened? or who laid the corner stone thereof;7 When the **morning stars sang together**, and all **the sons of God** shouted for joy?

You should understand that God Created this second earth age because of the falling away of Satan and God's children in the first Earth and Heaven age whereby Satan deceived one third of God's children into following him, (Rev. 12 : 4) and thus caused God to destroy that age and decree that the sons of God (as in you and me) would have to go through the womb, the water and the flesh with everyone on equal ground, innocent of the age that then was and free to choose who they will follow; God or Satan.

When some of God's children refused to do this and came to earth, without going through the womb and the water, (Possessing full knowledge of the age that then was) we begin to see where Satan's children, the fallen angels, (aliens) are trying to disrupt God's plan of salvation for all of His children.

Keep in mind that we are all made in the image of God and the Angels (our own Terrestrial selves), (Gen: 1: 26)

> Gen 6:1-2:1 And it came to pass, when men began to multiply on the face of the earth, and daughters were born unto them, 2 That the sons of God (not men) saw the daughters of men that they were fair; and they took them wives of all which they chose.

Without going through the flesh.

> Gen 6:4 **There were giants in the earth in those days**; and also after that, when **the sons of God** came in unto the daughters of men, and they bare children to them, the same became **mighty men which were of old**, men of renown.

These are the giants who had 6 fingers and 6 toes.

New subject:

> Zech 1:9 Then said I, O my lord, what are these? And the angel that talked with me said unto me, I will shew thee what these be.

> Zech 1:10-15 And the man that stood among the myrtle trees answered and said, These are they whom the LORD hath sent to walk to and fro through the earth.
> 11 And they answered the **angel of the LORD** that stood among the myrtle trees, and said, We have walked to and fro through the earth, and, behold, all the earth sitteth still, and is at rest.

Notice it says is at rest not peace like fat and extremely happy Jeshurun (Deut.32 15).

These are the watchers.

> 12 Then the **angel of the LORD answered** and said, O LORD of hosts, how long wilt thou not have mercy on Jerusalem and on the cities of Judah, against which thou hast had indignation these threescore and ten years?
> 13 And the LORD answered the **angel that talked** with me with good words and comfortable words.
> 14 So the angel that communed with me said unto me, Cry thou, saying, Thus saith the LORD of hosts; I am jealous for Jerusalem and for Zion with a great jealousy.
> 15 And **I am very sore displeased**

with the heathen that are at ease:
for I was but a little displeased,
and they helped forward the
affliction.

Another time:

Matt 1:20 But while he thought on
these things, behold, the **angel of
the Lord appeared unto him in a
dream**, saying, Joseph, thou son of
David, fear not to take unto thee
Mary thy wife: for that which is
conceived in her is of the Holy
Ghost (Spirit).

Acts 12:7 And, behold, the **angel of
the Lord came upon him**, and a light
shined in the prison: and he smote
Peter on the side, and raised him
up, saying, Arise up quickly. And
his chains fell off from his hands.

Rev 12:9
And the great dragon was cast
out, that old serpent, called the
Devil, and Satan, which deceiveth
the whole world: he was cast out
into the earth, and **his angels
were cast out with him**.

These are the fallen ones.

Jude 6 **And the angels which kept
not their first estate, but left
their own habitation,** he hath
reserved in everlasting chains
under darkness unto the judgment
of the great day.

1 Cor 6:3 Know ye not that we
shall judge angels? how much more
things that pertain to this life?

Eph 6:12 For **we wrestle not
against flesh and blood, but
against principalities, against
powers, against the rulers of the
darkness of this world, against
spiritual wickedness in high
places.**

What about the influx of the FALLEN
ANGELS, their taking daughters of Adam
as wives and the resulting children
i.e. GIANTS.

Giants:
Deut 3:11 For only Og king of Bashan
remained of the remnant of giants;
behold, his bedstead was a bedstead of
iron; is it not in Rabbath of the
children of Ammon? nine cubits was the
length thereof, and four cubits the
breadth of it, after the cubit of a man.

This giant's bed was about 13'6" long
and 6 feet wide.

Deut 2:11 Which also were accounted
giants, as the **Anakims**; but the
Moabites call them **Emims.**

Anakims: OT:6062 `Anaqiy (an-aw-kee');
patronymically from OT:6061; an Anakite
or descendant of Anak: OT:6059`anaq (aw-
nak'); a primitive root; properly, to
choke; used only as denominative from
OT:6060, to collar, i.e. adorn with a
necklace; figuratively, to fit out with
supplies: compass about as a chain,

furnish, liberally.

Emims:
OT:368 'Eymiym (ay-meem'); plural of
OT:367; **terrors**; Emim, an early
Canaanitish (or Maobitish) tribe: OT:367
'eymah (ay-maw'); or (shortened) 'emah
(ay-maw'); from the same as OT:366;
fright; concrete, an idol (as a
bugbear):OT:366 'ayom (aw-yome'); from
an unused root (meaning to frighten);
frightful: OT:367'eymah (ay-maw'); or
(shortened) 'emah (ay-maw'); from the
same as OT:366; fright; <u>**concrete, an**
idol</u> (as a bugbear):

In the Land of Og they worshiped the
Asherash. This is a pole shaped like a
male organ which was originally
worshiped as a symbol of life and later
combined with the multi breasted Goddess
of Fertility, Ishtar, and recently
perverted further and called Easter with
the Rabbit symbolizing fertility. These
people were idol worshipers, perverts
and ultimately perished.

Does Easter Island ring a bell ---
hello!
Let us not be willingly ignorant of what
we know is actually here. Giant, stone
or concrete type statues.

There was a second generation of giants
born and they are recorder in:

1 Chron 20:4-6 And it came to pass
after this, that there arose war at
Gezer with the Philistines; at which
time Sibbechai the Hushathite slew
Sippai, that was of the **children of**

63

the giant: and they were subdued.
5 And there was war again with the
Philistines; and Elhanan the son of
Jair slew Lahmi the **brother of
Goliath** the Gittite, whose spear
staff was like a weaver's beam.
6 And yet again there was war at
Gath, where was a man of great
stature, **whose fingers and toes were
four and twenty, six on each hand,
and six on each foot: and he also
was the son of the giant.**

Do you suppose that this might have
something to do with the Mark God placed
on Cain, like maybe a 6 or a 6 or a 6?

Could it be, that Satan's offspring
(seed) had sex with the fallen angels
and the 6th day tribes after Cain was
sent packing into the land of Nod (Gen.
3 16)for killing Abel?

In conclusion; We wrestle against
principalities and powers of wickedness
in high places. Against rulers of
darkness, deceivers with beguiling lips.

As there were two trees in the Garden of
Eden (in the beginning) there shall also
be two trees (two Christ's) at the end.
The false Christ, like the moon (with
only a reflection of the true light)
calling himself Christ and God and the
true Christ who comes **after** the 6th
trump, the 6th seal and the 6th vial. The
true Christ comes at the 7th trump, 7th
seal and 7th vial. Listen, if you hear
the thunders it means that the lightning
has already hit. And "I beheld Satan as
lightning fall from heaven" (Luke: 10:18)

We have the promises of the LORD that if we keep His word and fear (revere) Him not one hair on our heads will be hurt. (Luke: 21:18).

It is written also that Satan and his angels can only hurt those men without the seal of God in their foreheads, (Rev.: 9:4), which means that they must have some other seal like the mark of the beast or seal of Satan's lies and deceptions and perversions of the truth. If you would like to plow a little deeper please write to Kings Chapel or Shepherds chapel for their free booklet and or tape on the subject. The Plan of God and The Mark of the Beast respectively.

The NEPHILIM, or "Giants" of Genesis 6 &c.
(APPENDIX 25 of the COMPANION BIBLE)

The progeny of the fallen angels with the daughters of Adam are called in Genesis 6, Nephilim, which means fallen ones (from naphal, to fall). What these beings were can be gathered only from Scripture. They were evidently great in size, as well as in wickedness. They were superhuman, abnormal beings; and their destruction was necessary for the preservation of the human race and for the faithfulness of Yahveh's Word (Gen 3:15).
This is why the flood was brought "upon the world of the ungodly" (2 Pet 2:5) as prophesied by Enoch (Jude 14).

But we read of the Nephilim again in

Numbers 13:33: "there we saw the Nephilim, the sons of Anak, which come of the Nephilim". How, it may be asked, could this be, if they were all destroyed in the flood? The answer is contained in Gen. 6:4, where we read: "There were Nephilim in the earth in the earth in those days (i.e. in the days of Noah); and also AFTER THAT, when the sons of God came in unto the daughters of Adam, and they bare children unto them, the same became [the] mighty men (Heb. gibbor, the heroes) which were of old, men of renown" (lit. men of the name, i.e. who got a name and were renown for their ungodliness).

So that "after that", i.e. after the flood, there was a second irruption of these fallen angels, evidently smaller in number and more
limited in area, for they were for the most part confined to Canaan, and were in fact known as "the nations of Canaan". It was for the destruction of these, that the sword of Israel was necessary, as the flood had been before.

As to the date of this second irruption, it was evidently soon after it became known that the seed was to come through Abraham; for when he came out from Haran (Gen. 12:60 and entered Canaan, the significant fact is stated: "The Cananite was then (i.e. already) in the land". And in Gen. 14:5 they were already known as "Rephaim" and "Emim", and had established themselves at Ashteroth Karnaim and Shaveh Kiriathaim. In ch. 15:18-24 they are enumerated and named among the Canaanite peoples;

66

"Kenites, and the Kenizzites, and the Kadmonites, and the Hittites, and the Perizzites, and the Rephaims, and the Amorites, and the Girgashites, and the Jebusites" (Gen. 15:19-21; cp. Ex. 3:8, 17; 23:23; Deut. 7; 20:17; Josh. 12:8).

These were to be cut off, and driven out, and utterly destroyed (Deut. 20:17; Josh. 3:10). But Israel failed in this (Josh. 13:13; 15:63; 16:10; 17:18; Judg. 1:19-20, 28-36; 2:1-5; 3:1-7); and we know not how many got away to other countries to escape the general destruction. If this were recognized it would go far to solve many problems connected with Anthropology.

As to their other names, they were called Anakim, from one Anak which came of the Nephilim (Num. 13:23), and Rephaim, from Rapha, another notable one among them.

From Deut. 2:10, they were known by some as Emim, and Horim, and Zamzummim (v. 20-21) and Avim, &c.

As Rephaim they were well known, and are often mentioned: but, unfortunately, instead of this, their proper name, being preserved, it is variously translated as "dead", "deceased", or "giants". These Rephaim are to have no resurrection. This fact is stated in Isa. 26:14 (where the proper name is rendered "deceased", and v. 19, where it is rendered "the dead"). It is rendered "deceased" in Isa. 26:14. It is retained as a proper name "Rephaim" ten times (two being in the margin). Gen. 14:5;

67

15:20; Josh. 12:15 (marg.). 2 Sam 5:18, 22; 23:13; 1 Chron. 11:15; 14:9; 20:4 (marg.). Isa. 17:5.

In all other places it is rendered "giants", Gen. 6:4, Num. 23:33;, where it is Nephilim; and Job 16:14, where it is gibbor.

By reading all these passages the Bible student may know all that can be known about these beings.

It is certain that the second irruption took place before Gen. 14, for there the Rephaim were mixed up with five nations or people, which included Sodom and Gomorrha, and were defeated by the

four kings under Chedorlaomer. Their principal locality was evidently "Ashtaroth Karnaim"; while the Emim were in the plain of Kiriathaim (Gen.14:5).

Anak was a noted descendent of the Nephilim; and Rapha was another, giving their names respectively to different clans. Anak's father was Arba, the original builder of Hebron (Gen. 35:27, Josh. 15:13; 21:11); and this Palestine branch of the Anakim was not called Arbahim after him, but Anakim after Anak. They were great, mighty, and tall (Deut 2:10-11, 21-23; 9:2), evidently inspiring the ten spies with great fear (Num. 13:33). Og king of Bashan is described in Deut. 3:11.
Their strength is seen in "the giant cities of Bashan" today; and we know not how far they may have been utilized by Egypt in the construction of buildings,

which is still an unsolved problem.
Arba was rebuilt by the Khabiri or
confederates seven years before Zoan was
built by the Egyptian Pharaohs of the
nineteenth dynasty. See note on Num.
13:22 (if you have a Companion Bible).
If these Nephilim, and their branch of
Rephaim, were associated with Egypt, we
have an explanation of the problem which
has for ages perplexed all engineers, as
to how those huge stones and monuments
were brought together. Why not in Egypt
as well as in "the giant cities of
Bashan" which exist, as such, to this
day? Moreover, we have in these mighty
men, the "men of renown", the
explanation of the origin of the Greek
mythology. That mythology was no mere
invention of the human brain, but it
grew out of the traditions, and
memories, and legends of the doings of
that mighty race of beings; and was
gradually evolved out of the "heroes' of
Gen. 6:4. The fact that they were
supernatural in their origin formed an
easy step to their being regarded as the
demigods of the Greeks. Thus the
Babylonian "Creation Tablets", the
Egyptian "Book of the dead", the Greek
mythology, and heathen Cosmogonies,
which by some are set on an equality
with Scripture, or by others adduced in
support of it, are all the corruption
and perversion of primitive truths,
distorted in proportion as their origin
was forgotten, and their memories faded
away.

We have seen that there really are good
and bad angels. That there is a
controversy going on between Satan and

69

God. We will not escape choosing one
side or the other in this war for the
souls of God's children and we are all
HIS children. See, the Bible is more
than a book. It is a history of how
things are coming down in this final
generation. It tells us what happened in
the past as an example and story of how
it's going to happen again.

It is written:

> 1 Cor 10:11-12 Now all these things
> happened unto them for ensamples:
> and they are written for our
> admonition, upon whom the ends of
> the world are come.
> 12 Wherefore let him that thinketh
> he standeth take heed lest he fall.1
> Peter 4:12-13 Beloved, think it not
> strange concerning the fiery trial
> which is to try you, as though some
> strange thing happened unto you:13
> But rejoice, inasmuch as ye are
> partakers of Christ's sufferings;
> that, when his glory shall be
> revealed, ye may be glad also with
> exceeding joy. KJV

When we begin to see the TRUTH we find
peace.

Matt 10:26 Fear them not therefore: for
there is nothing covered, that shall not
be revealed; and hid, that shall not be
known.

Luke 10:19 Behold, I give unto you power to tread on serpents and scorpions, and over all the power of the enemy: and nothing shall by any means hurt you.

How do we get this power?

If you learn the WORD and rightly divide it as in really want to dig and check out the Hebrew and Greek words, metaphors and similitude's.

John 8:32 And ye shall know the truth, and the truth shall make you free. KJV

Chapter VI

What does 666 really mean?

Rev 13: 18 Here is <u>wisdom,</u> Let him that hath understanding <u>count</u> the <u>number</u> of the <u>beast:</u> for it is the <u>number of a man;</u> and his number is Six hundred three score and six.

Did you know that Satan has a mark and God also has a mark or seal here in the end times?

There were two trees in the Garden of Eden; the Tree of Life and the Tree of the knowledge of good and evil also known as death.

There were two sons born to Adam and Eve; Cain of the evil tree and Abel of Adam's seed.

Have you ever heard the expression, "Family Tree"?

There are two Jesus' or two Christ's in revelations, (One calling himself Christ and the real Christ) and throughout the book Just like there were two trees in the Garden of Eden; the tree of Life and the tree of Death.

The false Christ will appear on earth calling himself Christ and God sitting in the holy place.

That Jesus told us that He is the Alpha and the Omega, the beginning and the end (Rev. 1: 8).

Jesus didn't say He was next to the end. Why wouldn't one want to be here when Jesus returns at the end?

As it was in the beginning so it shall be in the end and there is nothing new under the sun.

Here is one of many examples of the mark God placed on Cain and his prodigy for our understanding and recognition.

1 Kings 10-14 **When the Queen of the South came to Solomon**, the smartest man on earth, and gave him of HER gifts, 666 pieces of gold. Why did she think she could approach Solomon?

Possibly because Solomon had been worshiping the idols and making sacrifices to the other gods of the many STRANGE women he had married. By these gifts Solomon told the Queen all that he had. Solomon's kingdom became the wealthiest in all the earth. Silver became like pebbles in the streets and they possibly even had gold toothpicks.

Look at the idol, image that king Nebuchadnezzar had set up (Dan. 3: 1-30) was 60cubits high and 6 cubits broad. They were to fall down and worship the image when the 6 instruments were played. Starting to get the idea of the 6's, which in Biblical numeric means the weakness of man.

73

Keep an eye on the 6th vial, the 6th seal and the 6th trump as we show exactly what Satan, the beast system and the false prophet will be doing during the tribulation. This is just before the 7th, vial 7th seal and 7 trumpets are blown, whereupon Christ returns.

Could it be that the Tribulation is not what we have been led to believe with death and destruction everywhere?

Could it be a time of Peace Peace and prosperity for everyone who worships the beast (One World System) and the Image that looks like Christ and speaks like the dragon?

Let's begin with the Mark of the Beast, his image and his number.

> REV 15: 2 And I saw as it were a sea of glass mingled with fire: and **them that had gotten the victory** over the **BEAST**, and over the **IMAGE**, and over his **MARK** and over **THE NUMBER OF HIS NAME,** stand on the sea of glass, having the harps of God.
> And they sing the song of Moses the servant of God, and the song of the Lamb, saying, Great and marvelous are Thy works, Lord God Almighty; just and true are Thy ways, Thou King of saints. Who shall not revere The, O Lord, and glorify Thy name? For Thou only art holy: for all nations shall come and worship before Thee; for Thy judgments are made manifest.

Victory over the; beast, image, mark and number. These **Five** show how the victory is obtained.
Five, means Grace in Biblical Mathematics by Ed. F. Vallowe, published by the Olive Press.

Let us properly divide God's word. Let's go to the Greek as translated into the New Testament from the Manuscripts.

(Rev 19:20) And the **Beast** was taken, and with him the **false Prophet** that wrought miracles before him, with which he deceived them that had received the **mark** of the beast, and them that worshiped his **image**.

So he used the Beast and False Prophet to deceive them that had received the mark (badge of servitude) of the beast and became apostate by worshiping his image.

Let us look up the word beast in Strongs Exhaustive Concordance as in the hidden beast system of Satan's four hidden dynasties; education, religion, economics and political. These hidden agenda systems correspond to the four horsemen in Rev.6-1

Beast: NT:2339 thera (thay'-rah); from ther (a wild animal, as game); hunting, i.e. (figuratively) **destruction:** - **trap**

Now look up false prophet who will stand in the Holy place claiming to be Christ and God. This is the false Christ presenting an image that he is Christ. (2Thes. 2: 1-4).

False Prophet: NT:5578 pseudoprophetes (psyoo-dop-rof-ay'-tace); from NT:5571 and NT:4396; a spurious prophet, i.e. pretended foreteller or **religious impostor**: NT:5571 pseudes (psyoo-dace'); from NT:5574; untrue, i.e. erroneous, **deceitful, wicked: KJV - false, liar**. NT:5574 pseudomai (psyoo'-dom-ahee); middle voice of an apparently primary verb; to **utter an untruth or attempt to deceive by falsehood**: KJV - falsely, lie.

Now let's look up the **meaning of: image**, mark, and number in which we are instructed to gain the victory over.

<u>**IMAGE:**</u> Strongs: 1504 i-kone, from 1503; <u>a likeness, i.e. (lit.), **statue,**</u> <u>**profile, or (fig.) representation,**</u> <u>**resemblance.**</u> 1503 i-ko; appar. a primary verb [Perh. akin to 1502 through the idea of faintness as a copy]1 to **resemble:-be alike**. 1502 i-ko appar. a primary verb; prop. to be weak i.e. <u>yield: give place.</u>

<u>**MARK:**</u> Rev 20: 4 his mark upon (in) their foreheads, where your brain is. Strongs: 5480 charagma, khar-ag-mah; from the same as 5482; a scratch or etching, i.e. <u>stamp (**as a badge of**</u> <u>**servitude**</u>), or <u>sculptured figure</u>

(statue); - graven, mark. 5482 charax, khar-ax; from (to sharpen, to a point; akin to 1125 through the idea of scratching); a stake, i.e. (by Impl.) a palisade or rampart (military mound for circumvallation in a siege) - trench. 1125 grapho graf-o; a primary verb; to "grave," espec. to write; fig. to describe - describe, write (-ing, -ten).

NUMBER: Strongs: 706 ar-ith-mos; from 142 ah-ee-ro; a prim verb; to lift; by impl. to take up or away; fig. to raise (the voice), keep in suspense (the mind), spec. to sail away (i.e weigh anchor); by Heb. [comp. 5375] to expiate sin: - away with, bear (up) carry, lift up, loose, **make to doubt, put away, remove,** take (away, up). 5375: naw-saw; a prim. root; to lift, in a great variety of applications,

We now know that the Beast means a hidden trap, like the four hidden dynasties: that the False Prophet is an impostor and a liar, that the image means be like, as in cast the likeness of Christ, that mark means badge of servitude and number means to make to doubt.

In order to have victory over these things one must know the truth about the Beast 's (System) hidden agenda and false prophet disguised as Christ. That we will not serve his false truths and lies while having no doubt as to who he really is, what their agenda is and what God's true plan of salvation is for His children.

How do we do this?

By knowing what God has to say and not what man has to say. By rightly dividing God's word and keeping man's grubby little hands out of it. More correctly put by Jesus. Beware of the Levin of the Pharisees and of the Sadducees (Matt 16-6).

Otherwise we will have the mark of the beast in our brains or foreheads and serve him with our right hand as in supporting his false doctrines and Bethavens (empty houses of God).

Now God's seal also in the forehead as in the brain.

> Rev 7:2-3 And I saw another **angel ascending from the east, having the seal of the living God**: and he cried with a loud voice to the four angels, to whom it was given to hurt the earth and the sea, 3 Saying, **Hurt not the earth, neither the sea, nor the trees, till we have sealed the servants of our God in their foreheads.**

What is the Seal of God? It is having the THUTH, THE KEY OF DAVID.

Example: what was the stone that David threw at Goliath that caused Goliath's deadly wound?

(Luke 11 28). Hint: David picked up 5 (Meaning grace in biblical numerics) stones (1 Sam 17: 40) from the brook of living waters (TRUTH) and hurled the one stone at Goliath (giant beast) which caused the deadly wound. Out of the mouths of babes. (Matt. 21: 16) See how all of God's word comes together. We shall go into more detail about this later on.

Rev 9:4 And it was commanded them that they should not hurt the grass of the earth, neither any green thing, neither any tree; **but only those men which have not the seal of God** in **their foreheads.**

Ezek 9:6 Slay utterly old and young, both maids, and little children, and women: but **come not near any man upon whom is the mark; and begin at my sanctuary.** Then they began at the ancient men which were before the house.

Why? Because you know God's true plan of salvation and you don't get deceived by the king's meat as in false doctrine.

Oh! Oh! Why are they to begin at the Sanctuary?

Could it be because they are not teaching the TRUTH? They are hirelings (John 10-12) and do not care for the sheep. They only care to Prophesy (teach) out of their own minds, things that God has not said and they do it for money (Eze.34-8) (Isaiah. 56-11).

Mark: Strongs (H 8427) Tavah, Taw-Vah; a prime root; **to mark out**, i.e. (prim.) scratch or (def.) imprint:--scrabble, set (s mark).

Iniquity: (H 5753) Strongs: avah, aw-vah; a prime root: to crook. Lit. or fig. (as follows):--do amiss, bow down, make crooked, commit iniquity, pervert, (do) perverse (-ly), trouble, x turn, do wickedly, do wrong.

Let us learn **who prevailed to open the seals**.

> Dan 12:4 But thou, O **Daniel, shut up the words, and seal the book, even to the time of the end**: many shall run to and fro, and knowledge shall be increased.
>
> **2 Tim 2:19** Nevertheless **the foundation of God standeth sure, having this seal**, The Lord knoweth them that are his. And, Let every one that nameth the name of Christ depart from iniquity.
>
> **Rev 5:5** And one of the elders saith unto me, Weep not: behold, the **Lion of the tribe of Juda, the Root of David, hath prevailed to open the book, and to loose the seven seals thereof.**

We now see that God's seal is applied to those who know the truth, depart from iniquity, keep God's words and

80

learn the difference between righteousness and unrighteousness, the holy and profane and the clean and unclean.

Now let's watch as John in Revelations is given the seals and then as Christ opens the seven seals and what He said about them.
Satan comes as the image of Christ at the 6th seal, 6th vial and 6th trump. This is when God's wrath boils over because His children do not want to hear about Him, His truths and His ways. They would rather believe a smoothie (stone) who speaks great swelling tales and empty stories and covers over the truth of God's words and God's outstretched arms, (Eze. 13: 20). God said He would send them strong delusion that they would believe a lie since they are not lovers of the truth but would rather get a warm fuzzy and call it religious.

In counting the stones worn smooth over a long period of time we are to look, see and know who the sons of Cain are and who controls the hidden dynasties of this world.

Note: When they crucified Christ He told them right to their face who's children they were. And to make a point they all yelled to release Barabbas which means Son of his father and a murderer. Who was the first murderer?

Let us do a little background by counting first.

Count the stones worn smooth over
A
Long period of time

Rev 13:18 Here is wisdom. Let him that hath understanding **count the number of the beast: for it is the number of a man;** and his number is Six hundred threescore and six.

Let us look up the meaning of the word Count and then look into the meaning of the stones.

Count: NT:5585 psephizo (psay-fid'-zo); from NT:5586; to use pebbles in enumeration, i.e. (generally) to compute: - count. (Biblesoft's New Exhaustive Strong's Numbers and Concordance with NT:5586 psephos (psay'-fos); from the same as NT:5584; a pebble (as worn smooth by handling), i.e. (by implication of use as a counter or ballot) a verdict (of acquittal) or ticket (of admission); a vote: - stone, voice.

David slew Goliath the Giant, who is a type of the antichrist, by picking up 5 (Grace in biblical numeric) smooth stones from the brook of living waters and heritage and threw one at the giant. What is going on with this?

What is the stone that David hurled that caused the deadly wound?
OR
Was it something David said to the Giant, Beast, Offspring of the Fallen Angels and type of Antichrist?

David:

1 Sam 17:40 And he (David) took his staff in his hand, and chose him **five smooth stones** out of the **brook,** **(of living waters and stone of descent by inheritance and covenant of the LORD)** and put them in a shepherd's bag which he had, even in a scrip; and his **sling (used for slinging the circular light of truth)** was in his hand: and he drew near to the Philistine.

Brook:OT:5157 nachal (naw-khal'); a primitive root; to inherit (as a [figurative] mode of descent), or (generally) to occupy; causatively, to **bequeath,** or (generally) distribute, instate:

To Sling:OT:7049 qala` (kaw-lah'); a primitive root: to sling: also to carve (as if a **circular motion, or into light forms**):V - carve, sling (out)

David speaking to the Idolatrous image of the beast, the fallen one (Philistines), (offspring of fallen angels).

Sam 17:46 This day will the LORD deliver thee into mine hand; and I will smite thee, and take thine head from thee; and I will give the carcases of the host of the Philistines this day unto the fowls of the air, and to the wild beasts of the earth; **that all the earth may know that there is a God in Israel.**

Philistine: OT:6297 Carcases: peger (peh'gher); from OT:6296; a carcase (as limp), whether of man or beast; figuratively, an **idolatrous image:**

1 Sam 17:47 **And all this assembly shall know that the LORD saveth not with sword and spear**: for **the battle is the LORD's, and he will give you into our hands.**

David spoke the truth and then followed it up with faith and action in that faith trusting that the Lord would deliver.

1 Sam 17:49 And David put his hand in his bag, and took thence **a stone(Christ, the word of God)** and slang it, and smote the Philistine in his forehead, that the stone sunk into his forehead; and he fell upon his face to the earth.

We see that David brought down the giant, beast, terror, with the stone of Grace, (Christ—the living word of God).

You see David knew the truth and when he spoke it to the false one it brought him down.

Let's go back to the seven vials and seven seals.

Who can open the seven seals, vials and trumps?

Daniel was told to seal up the book until the time of the end?

Many say the book is sealed and can't be understood.

Lets look and "see".

Mark 13:4-6 Tell us, when shall these things be? and **what shall be the sign when all these things shall be fulfilled?**
As in what will it be like when you return?

SEVEN SEALS

Rev 5:8-9 And when he had taken the book, the four beasts and four and twenty elders fell down before the Lamb, having every one of them harps, and golden vials full of odours, which are The prayers of saints. 9 And they sung a new song, saying, Thou art worthy to take the book, and to open the seals thereof: for thou wast slain, and hast redeemed us to God by thy blood out of every kindred, and tongue, and people, and nation;

FIRST SEAL   John in Revelations:

Rev 6:2 And I saw, and behold a white horse: and he that sat on him had a **bow; and a crown was given unto him: and he went forth conquering, and to conquer.**

BOW: NT:5115 toxon (tox'-on); from the base of NT:5088; a bow (apparently as the **simplest fabric**):

CROWN: NT:4735 stephanos (stef'-anos); from an apparently primary stepho (to twine or wreathe); a chaplet (as a **badge of royalty**, a prize in the public games or a symbol of honor generally; but more conspicuous and elaborate than the simple fillet, NT:1238), literally or figuratively:

CONQUER AND CONQUERING: is the same word in Greek. NT:3528   nikao (nik-ah'-o); from NT:3529; to subdue (literally or figuratively): - **conquer, overcome, prevail, get the victory**.

We have a cheap imitation, like a man standing in purple and scarlet priests robe, preaching and teaching great things that really feel good, standing in a huge awesome building with stained glass. Surely this great man "of god" wouldn't deceive us? Would he?

The LAMB who is worthy will tell us.

FIRST SEAL OPENED: Jesus speaking. Mark 13:5-6 And Jesus answering them began to say, **Take heed lest any man deceive** you: 6 For many shall come in my name, saying, I am Christ; (Christian) and shall deceive many.

SECOND SEAL: John in Revelaitons. Rev 6:4 And there went out another horse that was red: and power was given to him that sat thereon to **take peace from the earth, and that they should kill one another: and there was given unto him a great sword.**

Mark 13:7 Jesus Speaking.

7 And when ye shall hear of wars and rumours of wars, be ye not troubled: for such things must needs be; but the end shall not be yet.

Wars and rumors of wars, WWI and WWII and then rumors of nuclear annihilation. The COLD War.

THIRD SEAL: John in Revelations.

Rev 6:6 And I heard a voice in the midst of the four beasts say, **A measure of wheat for a penny, and three measures of barley for a penny; and see thou hurt not the oil and the wine.**

A penny was a days earnings then. A loaf of bread for a days wages. How much do you really have left after you pay your mortgage, car payment, credit cards and taxes? That is your days wage.

THIRD SEAL: Jesus speaking.

Mark 13:8 For nation shall rise against nation, and kingdom against kingdom: and there shall be earthquakes in divers places, and there shall be famines and troubles: **these are the beginnings of sorrows.** As in birth pains.

RISE: NT:1453 egeiro (eg-i'-ro); probably akin to the base of NT:58 (through the idea of collecting one's faculties); to waken NT:58 agora (ag-or-ah'); from ageiro (to gather; probably akin to NT:1453); properly, the town-square (as a place of public resort); by implication, **a market or thoroughfare: - market (-place),** street.

AGAINST: NT:1909 epi (ep-ee'); a primary preposition; properly, meaning superimposition (of time, place, order, etc.) NT:1909 - about (the times), above, after, **against, among, as long as (touching), at, beside**, have charge of, (be-, [wherefore-]), in (a place, as much as, the time of, -to), (because) of, (up-) on (behalf of), over, (by, for) the space of, through (-out), (un-) to (-ward), with. In compounds it retains essentially the same import, at, upon, etc. (literally or figuratively).

Nation standing alongside nation in the market place. This is NAFTA and the NWO with free world trade. Nation is referring to what we call the third world nations and Kingdoms are the Free world Christian Kingdoms.

FOURTH SEAL: John in Revelations.

Rev 6:8 And I looked, and behold a pale horse: and his name that sat on him was Death, and Hell followed with him. And <u>power was given unto them over the fourth part of the earth, to kill with sword, and with hunger, and with death, and with the beasts of the earth.</u>

The four parts of the Earth and the Beasts of the Earth are the same as the four horsemen and the four hidden dynasties of; Religion, Economics, Politics and Education, whereby Satan's children have deceived and misguided God's children into believing their false teachings. This same thing happened to Eve in the Garden.

Famine and Hunger causes physical and spiritual starvation and then death both spiritually and physically.

Amos 8:11-12 Behold, the days come, **saith the Lord GOD, that I will send a famine in the land, not a famine of bread, nor a thirst for water, but of hearing the words of the LORD:** 12 And they shall wander from sea to sea, and from the north even to the east, **they shall run to and fro to seek the word of the LORD, and shall not find it.**

Their power to kill with the sword means using the Word of God to deceive and spin into a false truth that kills the soul, and if this isn't enough they starve the children by teaching lies and traditions that make void the true saving grace of our LORD. This causes death to the spiritual man within as God's children are led to worship false gods, gods that came newly up by men and have no life in them and the Beasts of the Earth like the Banking and Economic System bringing God's children into Debt and Bondage to them.

FIFTH SEAL: John in Revelations.

Rev 6:9-10 And when He had opened the
fifth seal, I saw under the altar the
souls of them that were slain for the
word of God, and for the testimony
which they held: 10 And they cried
with a loud voice, saying, **How long,
O Lord, holy and true, dost thou not
judge** and avenge our blood on them
that dwell on the earth?

Jesus speaking:

Mark 13:9-13 But take heed to
yourselves: for they shall deliver
you up to councils; and in the
synagogues ye shall be beaten: and
ye shall be brought before rulers
and kings for my sake, for a
testimony against them.10 And the
gospel must first be published among
all nations.

God will see to it that all will hear
the Gospel in their own TONGUE as the
Holy Spirit speaks through those who are
delivered up.

11 But when they shall lead you,
and deliver you up, take no thought
beforehand what ye shall speak,
neither do ye premeditate: but
whatsoever shall be given you in
that hour, that speak ye: for it is
not ye that speak, but the Holy
Ghost. =(Spirit)

Now we come to the 6th seal. This is Satan's appearing with all signs and wonders.

Rev 6:12-17; 12 And I beheld when he had opened the **sixth seal**, and, lo, there was a great earthquake; and the sun became black as sackcloth of hair, and the moon became as blood; 13 And the <u>stars of heaven fell unto the earth</u>, even as a fig tree casteth her untimely figs, when she is shaken of a mighty wind. 14 And the heaven departed as a scroll when it is rolled together; and every mountain and island were moved out of their places. 15 And the kings of the earth, and the great men, and the rich men, and the chief captains, and the mighty men, and every bondman, and every free man, hid themselves in the dens and in the rocks of the mountains; 16 And said to the mountains and rocks, Fall on us, and <u>hide us from the face of him that sitteth on the throne, and from the wrath of the Lamb:</u> 17 For the great day of his wrath is come; and who shall be able to stand?

God's wrath is the sending of the Antichrist to come and chastise his children of disobedience by taking all into captivity so that in the end they might know who LORD GOD ALMIGHTY is. God will show signs and wonders as He did before Pharaoh in Egypt so that all may know that he alone is LORD and there is none other.

Jesus opening the 6th seal.

SIXTH SEAL: Jesus speaking

Matt:13 12 Now the brother shall
betray the brother to death,
(Death is one of Satan's names.
He will be calling himself
Christ and God when he appears
this time) and the father the
son; and children shall rise up
against their parents, and shall
cause them to be put to death.
13 And ye shall be hated of all
men for my name's sake: but he
that shall endure unto the end,
the same shall be saved.
Because they will believe Satan
is Christ. Mark 13:14-22 14 But
when ye shall see the
abomination of desolation,
spoken of by Daniel the prophet,
standing where it ought not,
(let him that readeth
understand,) then let them that
be in Judea flee to the
mountains:

Lets go to Daniel and the setting up of
the false one.

First lets see what Daniel the Prophet
said that Christ is referring to?

Dan 12:11-13
11 And from the time that the daily
sacrifice shall be taken away, and
the abomination that maketh desolate
set up, there shall be a thousand
two hundred and ninety days.
12 **Blessed is he that waiteth**, and

92

cometh to the thousand three hundred
and five and thirty days.
13 But go thou thy way till the end
be: for thou shalt rest, and stand
in thy lot at the end of the days.

The taking away of the daily sacrifice
is that they will be taking communion to
the False Christ instead of the TRUE
Christ. The abomination is Satan calling
himself Christ and God, sitting in the
Holy Temple which really belongs to GOD
ALMIGHTY.
Bad move buddy!

**This does not say blessed is he that is
raptured out of here. It says blessed is
he who waited until the end.**

Now speaking of the Anti - instead of
Christ and his false angels of light
disguised as ministers of righteousness
(2Cor. 11:14-15).

Dan 11:31- And arms shall stand on
his part, and **they shall pollute the
sanctuary of strength, and shall
take away the daily sacrifice**, and
**they shall place the abomination
that maketh desolate**. 32 And such as
do wickedly against the covenant
shall he corrupt by flatteries: **but
the people that do know their God
shall be strong,** and do exploits.

Back to Jesus speaking:

Mark 13: 15 And let him that is on
the housetop not go down into the
house, neither enter therein, to
take any thing out of his house:16

93

And let him that is in the field not
turn back again for to take up his
garment. 17 But woe to them that are
with child, and to them that give
suck in those days! 18 And pray ye
that your flight be not in the
winter.

Don't even pack your bags, time is that
short.

Woe to those that are impregnated with
Satan's false doctrine, thinking he is
the true Christ, worshiping Satan's
image and are nursing along Satan's
deceptions. Pray that you are not
harvested out of season like raptured
before the true Christ returns.

19 For **in those days shall be
affliction (G-2347:thlipsis,
anguish, persecution) such as was
not from the beginning of the
creation** which God created unto this
time, neither shall be. 20 And
except that the Lord had shortened
those days, no flesh should be
saved: but for the elect's sake,
whom he hath chosen, he hath
shortened the days.

21 And then **if any man shall say to
you, Lo, here is Christ; or, lo, he
is there; believe him not**: 22 For
**false Christs and false prophets
shall rise, and shall shew signs and
wonders**, to seduce, if it were
possible, even the elect.

SEVENTH SEAL:

Rev 8:1-2 And when he had opened the seventh seal, there was silence in heaven about the space of half an hour. 2 And I saw the seven angels which stood before God; and to them were given **seven trumpets**.

Read how Joshua took Jericho and the 7 trumpets along with the final shout on the 7th day as the priests blew all 7 trumpets. (Joshua 6: 3-6)

Jesus Speaking of the 7th and last seal, trumpet and vial.

Mark 13:24-26 24 But in those days, **after that tribulation**, the sun shall be darkened, and the moon shall not Give her light, 25 And the stars of heaven shall fall, and the powers that are in heaven shall be shaken. 26 And **then shall they see the Son of man coming in the clouds with great power and Glory.**

1 Thess 4:16 For the Lord himself shall descend from heaven with a shout, with the voice of the archangel, and with the trump of God: and the dead in Christ shall rise first KJV Amen

Chapter VII

Speaking in Tongues

We will show, by rightly dividing the word of God, that the tongue (s) spoken on Penticost Day was: 1. After a rushing mighty wind came from Heaven, 2. That they saw cloven tongues that looked like fire (lightning) came from Heaven and sat on each of the Apostles, 3. Everyone that saw and heard this were from all languages (tongues) around the Earth and 4. Everyone's first reaction was amazement and confusion as they couldn't understand what just happened and how they all heard these men speak in their native tongue.

Acts 2:1:1 And when the day of Pentecost was fully come, they were all with one accord in one place. Acts 2:2-2 And suddenly there came a sound from heaven as of a **rushing mighty wind**, and it filled all the house where they were sitting. 3 And **there appeared unto them cloven tongues like as of fire**, and it sat upon each of them. 4 And they were all filled with the Holy Ghost, and began to speak with other tongues, (NT 1100 Languages) as the Spirit gave them utterance. (NT5350 Speak clearly) KJV

Fire: Strongs: (G:4442): pur (poor); a primary word; "fire" (literally or figuratively, **specifically, lightning**):

96

Tongues: Strongs Exhaustive Concordance: (G:1100) glossa (gloce-sah'); of uncertain affinity; the tongue; by implication, **a language (specially, one naturally unacquired)**:- tongue.

> 6. Now when this was noised abroad, the multitude came together, and were confounded, because that every man heard them speak in his own language. 7 And they were all amazed and marvelled, saying one to another, Behold, are not all these which speak Galilaeans? 8 **And how hear we every man in our own tongue, wherein we were born?**

If you do not hear a rushing mighty wind and see cloven tongues of fire over those who are speaking and hear them speak clearly in your native dialect, then you are being deceived as well as the person who is speaking for he is speaking out of his own mind and deceiving himself as well.

Beginning with Pentecost day and the supernatural entrance of the Holy Spirit speaking through the LORD'S witnesses.

First a little foundation from the Holy Sprit by Timothy.

> **1 Tim 6:19-21**
> 19 **Laying up in store for themselves a good foundation against the time to come,** that they may lay hold on eternal life. 20 O Timothy, keep that

which is committed to thy trust,
avoiding profane and vain
babblings, and oppositions of
science falsely so called:
21 Which some professing have
erred concerning the faith.
Grace be with thee. Amen.

Vain Babblings: Strongs: (G:2757)
kenophonia (ken-of-o-nee'-ah); from a
presumed compound of NT:2756 and
NT:5456; **empty** sounding, i.e. **fruitless
discussion**:

Vain: Strongs: (G:2756) kenos (kenos'); apparently a **primary word; empty**
(literally or figuratively): - **empty,**
(in) vain.

Babblings: Strongs: (G:5456)phone (fo-
nay'); probably akin to NT:5316 through
the idea of disclosure; a tone
(**articulate, bestial or
artificial**); by implication, **an
address (for any purpose), saying or
language**: - **noise, sound, voice.**

> **2 Tim 2:15-16**
> 15 Study to shew thyself
> approved unto God, a workman
> that needeth not to be ashamed,
> rightly dividing the word of
> truth.
> 16 **But shun profane and vain
> babblings: for they will
> increase unto more ungodliness.**

This is saying, Avoid vain or empty
Babblings.

Babble means confusion and babblings comes from the Greek fo-nay from which we derive our word phony.

Many will refer to 1 Corinthians regarding spiritual gifts of: Prophesying and speaking in Tongues=naturally unacquired languages as their justification for babbling in their pride of the flesh.

This is the part that they left out.

1 Cor 14:27-28 If any man speak in an unknown tongue, (language) let it be by two, or at the most by three, and that by course; and let one interpret. 28 **But if there be no interpreter, let him keep silence in the church**; and let him speak to himself, and to God. KJV

Why? Because God confounded all languages in Babylon and God understands all languages.

Looking at JOEL the Prophet and what the Holy Spirit spoke through Joel we should read the whole book of Joel.
Herein Joel is proclaiming the wonderful works of the LORD as he shows exactly what God's plan of salvation is and what is going to happen in the latter times.

Joel 2:1 Blow ye the trumpet in Zion, and sound an alarm in my holy mountain: let all the inhabitants of the land tremble: for the day of the LORD cometh, for it is nigh at hand;

Sound the WARNING!
THE FALSE CHRIST IS COMING CLAIMING TO BE CHRIST AND YOU ARE GOING INTO CAPTIVITY. YOU ARE GOING THROUGH THE TRIBULATION.

Do not be unwise, as the five virgins of (Matt. 25:1) who did not have enough oil of truth in their lamps (word of God) to SEE through the coming darkness and flood of lies.

This is a spiritual and supernatural battle that is coming for your soul not flesh, so get ready.

> Joel 2:15 Blow the trumpet in Zion, <u>sanctify a fast,</u> call a solemn assembly: Joel 2:21 Fear not, O land; be glad and rejoice: for the LORD will do great things. Joel 2:32 And it shall come to pass, that whosoever shall call on the name of the LORD shall be delivered: for in mount Zion and in Jerusalem shall be deliverance, as the LORD hath said, and in the remnant whom the LORD shall call.

God is not the author of confusion (1 Cor 14:33).

Did God's word say that whosoever speaketh in a babbling tongue shall be saved? **NO!**

Let's us see what the LORD said:

John 6:47 Verily, verily, I say unto you, **He that believeth on me hath everlasting life.** **John 10:9** **I am the door: by me if any man enter in, he shall be saved,** and shall go in and out, and find pasture. **Acts 4:12** Neither is there salvation in any other: **for there is none other name under heaven** given among men, **whereby we must be saved.**

Chapter VIII

What is the Rapture doctrine and why is it not true?

We have multiple witnesses.

> Rev 22:13 I am Alpha and Omega, the beginning and the end, the **first and the last.**

Last means last not next to last.

Jesus now speaking.

> Matt 10:22 And ye shall be hated of all men for my name's sake: but he that **endureth to the end** shall be saved.

Endure to the end means; BE LEFT BEHIND IN THE GREEK: NT:5278 hupomeno (hoop-om-en'-o); from NT:5259 and NT:3306; to **stay under (behind)**, i.e. remain; figuratively, to undergo, i.e. bear (trials), have fortitude, persevere:

> Matt 24:13 But he that shall endure unto the end, the same shall be saved.

> Mark 13:13 And ye shall be hated of all men for my name's sake: but he that shall endure unto the end, the same shall be saved.

> Rev 2:26 And he that overcometh, and keepeth my works unto the end, to him will I give power over the nations:

Mark 13:24-26 But in those days, **after that tribulation,** the sun shall be darkened, and the moon shall not give her light, 25 And the stars of heaven shall fall, and the powers that are in heaven shall be shaken. 26 **And then** (after that) **shall they see the Son of man coming in the clouds** with great power and glory.

Does this sound like we will be gone before the tribulation?

Lets take a quick lesson in math and count the seals.
We will start with the last seal here so we get the idea. This is the 7th seal as in Mark 13, Matt. 24 and Rev. 8.

Rev 8:1-2 And when he had opened the seventh seal, there was silence in heaven about the space of half an hour. 2 And I saw the seven angels which stood before God; and to them were given **seven trumpets**.

There is a reason for this?

Heb 13:8 Jesus Christ the same Yesterday, and to day, and for ever. KJV

Lets look at Joshua (Yeshua) and what God instructed him to do.

Josh 6:3-4 And ye shall compass the city, all ye men of war, and go round about the city once. Thus shalt thou do six days. 4 And seven priests shall bear before the ark seven trumpets of rams' horns: and the seventh day ye shall compass the city seven times, and the priests shall blow with the (7) trumpets.

Josh 6:5 And it shall come to pass, that when they make a long blast with the ram's horn, and **when ye hear the sound of the trumpet, all the people shall shout with a great shout;** and the wall of the city shall fall down flat, and the people shall ascend up every man straight before him.

How do we suppose that the LORD will come and we will gather back to Him?

Rev 8:2 And I saw the seven angels which stood before God; and to them were given **seven trumpets.** KJV

1 Thes 4:16 **For the Lord himself shall descend from heaven with a shout, with the voice of the archangel, and with the trump (et) of God:** and the dead in Christ shall rise first:

This means the 7th trumpet, not the 5th or the 6th.

Who can open the seven seals, vials and trumpets?

Daniel was told to seal up the book until the time of the end?

Many say the book is sealed and can't be understood.

Lets look and "see".

Rev 5:8-9 And when he had taken the book, the four beasts and <u>four and twenty elders fell down before the</u> **Lamb,** having every one of them harps, and golden vials full of odours, which are the prayers of saints. 9 And they sung a new song, saying, **Thou art worthy to take the book, and to open the seals** thereof: <u>for thou wast slain, and hast redeemed us to God by thy blood</u> out of every kindred, and tongue, and people, and nation; KJV

We know who can open the (7) seals and reveal the truth to us. These words were spoken by Jesus to His disciples who went to Him privately and enquired as they wanted to learn from Him and not man. Read them for yourself; Matthew 24, Mark 13 and Luke 21. In Luke, Jesus was speaking to those in the Synagogue or Church as well.

Mark 13:4-6 Tell us, when shall these things be? and **what shall be the sign when all these things shall be fulfilled?**

As in, what will it be like when you return and we are gathered back to you?

Look and see the meaning of the seals as revealed by the Lamb who is worthy to open them.

We go into much more detail about this in Chapter 6 regarding the Number 666 and the Seal of the Living God.

> Mark 13:5 And Jesus answering them began to say, Take heed lest any man deceive you:
> (Seal # 1 **Warning!**)
>
> Mark 13:6 For many shall come in my name, saying, I am Christ; and shall deceive many. KJV

(**Seal # 2** calling themselves Christians and Ministers of righteousness while ripping off the people with white washed walls of false hope and rules made up by man, not God and not the truth that sets us free indeed).

Mark 13: 7 **Seal # 3** Wars and rumors of wars like the cold war we all heard about for many years with USSR and the Iron curtain.

Mark 13: 8 **Seal # 4** Nation shall rise against Nation. Properly translated from Greek rise against means stand along side of in the market place as in NAFTA, IMF and WTO.

Mark 13: 9-10 **Seal # 5 Mark** 13:Vs. 9-11 comes betrayal of brothers, delivering into the synagogues of those who have spoken truth from the word of God, their browbeating by angry brothers who have been deceived and refuse to believe the truth, and then the speaking of the two witnesses of God, leading into the 6th seal.

Mark 13: 11-23 # 6 SEAL AS IN 666   6th SEAL, 6th TRUMPET AND 6th VIAL.

THE LORD HAS NOT RETURNED YET !

Mark 13: Vs 14 **# 6 seal**: Now the abomination of desolation standing in the Holy Place spoken of by Daniel the Prophet is the False Prophet, False Image, calling himself Christ and God. (2Thes.2-4) Followed by his miracles and the great apostasy (Falling Away), where all believe the strong delusion, (The Image that Satan is Christ and God).

 # 7 Seal vs. 26 then shall they see the son of man coming in the clouds with great glory. TO SAVE HIS CHILDREN.

1 Thes. 4:16 **For the Lord himself shall descend from heaven with a shout, with the voice of the archangel, and with the trump (et) of God:** and the dead in Christ shall rise first:

LET US GO INTO MUCH MORE DEPTH AND MANY MORE WITNESSES ABOUT THE RAPTURE DECEPTION FROM THE WORD OF GOD.

We can trace the origin of the Rapture theory to Glasgow, Scotland, to the year 1830 when Margaret MacDonald, a "Christian" woman, had a vision (dream) where the Lord descended in the clouds and calls His saints to rise up and meet Him in the air. Although She said that the vision felt evil it holds some truth that at the sound of the 7th trumpet it is written. (1 Thes. 4-15) This is speaking about belief in Christ's resurrection as well as ours. They hang on this and leave out that it says "THEN WE WHICH REMAIN" (means left behind in Greek). Nevertheless, in order to trap the heathen into going to church this theory sounded good, though not Biblical it was adopted by some churches. Gone when the battle begins. Contrary to the Bible, they preach Peace and safety and they leave out the TRUTH that the False Christ is coming first, you are going through the tribulation and you are going into captivity to him and his system.

The Bible even tells us Why many believe this. 1. They are children of disobedience. 2. They do not seek and cherish God's TRUTH and 3. For this reason God said that HE would send them strong delusion that they would believe a lie.

Our military would call you a deserter, worthy of death. Others would call you a coward. What do you think God will call you?

Here is what God thinks about those who preach the Rapture doctrine.

Ezek 13:20 Wherefore thus saith the Lord GOD; Behold, **I am against** your pillows, wherewith ye there hunt the souls to make them fly, and I will tear them from your arms, and will let the souls go, even the souls that ye hunt to make them fly.

Pillows: OT:3680 kacah (kaw-saw'); a primitive root; properly, to plump, i.e. fill up hollows; by implication, to cover (for clothing or secrecy):

In other words covering God's outstretched saving arms.

Why would God tell us to put on the gospel armour to stand against the devil if we are not going to be here?

Eph 6:11 Put on the whole armour of God, that ye may be able to stand against the wiles of the devil. Eph 6:13 Wherefore take unto you the whole armour of God, **that ye may be able to withstand in the evil day,** and having done all, to stand.

Let us go to the second letter Paul wrote whereby he cleared up any misunderstandings about his first letter to the Thes. Like don't let his first letter trouble you about when we gather back to Christ.

(2 Th 2:1-2) Now we beseech you, brethren, by the coming of our Lord Jesus Christ, and by our gathering together unto Him, {2} **That ye be not soon shaken in**

mind, or be troubled, neither by
spirit, nor by word, nor by
letter as from us, as that the
day of Christ is at hand.

Shaken: NT:4531 saleuo (sal-yoo'-o);
from NT:4535; **to waver,** i.e. agitate,
rock, topple or (by implication)
destroy; figuratively, to disturb,
Incite:

> (2 Th 2:3) Let no man deceive you
> by any means: for that day shall
> not come, except there come a
> **falling away** first, and that man
> of sin be revealed, the **son of
> perdition;**

Falling away: From Strongs: NT:646
apostasia (ap-os-tas-ee'-ah); feminine
of the same as NT:647; **defection from
truth** (properly, the state)
["**apostasy**"]: falling away, **forsake.**

Falling away is not the rapture of the
church. Belief in the rapture is some
of the falling away (the apostasia—
defection from truth) The Greek is very
specific and defines it as Apostasy,
which means to turn from one's
professed beliefs.

**Who is the son of perdition that shall
be revealed?**

Perdition: NT:684 apoleia (ap-o'-li-a);
from a presumed derivative of NT:622;
ruin or loss (physical, spiritual or
eternal): - **damnable** (-nation),
destruction, die, perdition, **perish,**
pernicious ways, waste.

This son of perdition is satan. The only son (Ref. 9 11 **Apollyon**) who has been sentenced to perish, whose name is death. He was in the garden of Eden who caused death when Eve ate of his doctrine and was seduced. You can read about the description of the son who is sentenced to perish in Ezekiel 28.

Oh! Short side trip.

Satan does not have a red flannel suit and a pitchfork. He is the most beautiful Child God created with wisdom and knowledge (Ezekiel:28 12).

He was supposed to protect the rest of God's children covering of the mercy seat as high priest. Satan was sentenced to perish, because he deceived 1/3 of God's children in the first Earth and Heaven age with his false doctrines and idols. This is the root reason why we are here in this flesh Earth and Heaven age. Same MO in this Age (Eon). Hidden agendas, false teachings, bondage of the mind, spirit and body.

Revelation 9:11, Satan is given the name Apollyon. NT:623 **Apolluon** (ap-ol-loo'-ohn); active participle of NT:622; a destroyer (i.e. Satan): This has the same base root in the Greek as perdition.

(2 Th 2:4) Who opposes and exalteth himself above all that is called God, or that is worshipped; so that he as God sitteth in the temple of God, showing himself that he is God.

Another witness in Isaiah 14: 12, when Satan appears as the fake morning star and sits on Mt. Zion, in the Temple, claiming to be The Most High God.

Lets look at another witness of Satan's method of operation as he deceives the whole earth.

> Rev 13:13-14) And he doeth great wonders, so that he maketh fire come down from heaven on the earth in the sight of men, {14} And deceiveth them that dwell on the earth by the means of those miracles which he had power to do in the sight of the beast; saying to them that dwell on the earth, that they should make an image to the beast, which had the wound by a sword, and did live.

Jesus Speaking to the disciples.

> (2 Th 2:5-7) Remember ye not, that, when I was yet with you, I told you these things? {6} And now ye know what withholdeth that he might be revealed in his time. {7} For the mystery of iniquity doth already work: **only he who now letteth** will let, <u>until he be taken out of the way</u>.

Many teach that this "he" that is taken out of the way is the church in the so-called "rapture". Christ is a spiritual Husband returning for a spiritual bride. Christ is not returning to take a man (he), but a wife (she). The word letteth in the Greek is very important that you understand.

112

letteth: (G2722 katecho) = to **hold fast**. Katecho is a transitive verb, the object must be supplied. The subject is Satan, the object is satan's position in heaven (Eph 6:12) from where he will be cast out to earth (Revelation 12:7-10) at the sixth trumpet, when Michael who holds Satan in heaven until he receives orders from God to step out of the way and that it's time to cast him down to earth.

When did the walls of Jericho come tumbling down? (Joshua 6: 4-7) **When the seven Priests blew the seven trumpets on the seventh day (777).** Satan comes in Rev. at the 6th seal, the 6th vial and the 6th trumpet (666) The 7th has not been blown yet and will not until Christ is on His way and the walls come down between Heaven and Earth

> (2 Th 2:8-9) And then shall that Wicked be revealed, whom the Lord shall consume with the spirit of his mouth, and shall destroy with the brightness of His coming: {9} **Even him, whose coming is after the working of Satan** with all power and signs and lying wonders,

Satan's role as the false Messiah, along with his one world system (the four seals and four horsemen of Revelations) will be destroyed at Christ's return (Rev 19:20). Satan with all his power and signs and lying wonders which are the supernatural miracles he performs in Revelation 13. Also; Mat.24.

Mark 13:22. (2 Th 2:10) And with all deceivableness of unrighteousness in **them that perish; because they received not the love of the truth,** that they might be saved.

If you still refuse to believe the truth from God's mouth then this is what God says he is going to do. Ever say to your child, "keep screaming and jumping around like that and I'll give you something to jump around and scream about"?

(2 Th 2:11-12) And for this cause God shall send them strong delusion, that they should believe a lie: {12} **That they all might be damned** who believed not the truth, but had pleasure in unrighteousness.

Because God loves us so much He has sent the spirit of slumber upon many of His children. The spirit of slumber is placed on many of God's children so that they will not be held accountable. They will be taught in the millenium (Ezek: 44).

Spirit of slumber: NT:2659 katanuxis (kat-an'-oox-is); from NT:2660; a prickling (sensation, as of the limbs asleep), i.e. (by implication [perhaps by some confusion with NT:3506 or even with NT:3571]) stupor (lethargy): Rom 11:8, Isaiah 29:8-12.

(2 Th 2:13-14) But we are bound to give thanks alway to God for you, brethren beloved of the Lord, because God hath from the beginning chosen you to salvation through **sanctification of the Spirit and belief of the truth**: {14} Whereunto he called you by our gospel, to the obtaining of the glory of our Lord Jesus Christ.

If you love the truth then you will love God's words and not man's words. Remember Christ's first warning.

Luke 21:8 And he said, **Take heed that ye be not deceived**: for many shall come in my name, saying, I am Christ; and the time draweth near: **go ye not therefore after them.**

All will be rewarded according to your works.

Rev 22:11 He that is unjust, let him be unjust still: and he which is filthy, let him be filthy still: and he that is righteous, let him be righteous still: and he that is holy, let him be holy still.

Chapter IX

What does Easter really mean
And
What does Passover really mean?

I can't understand why, when I say I have been to Passover service, most people as well as those who call themselves Christians look at me perplexed and ask if I'm Jewish? Well, are all Christian's Jews or are all Jews Christians?

If you call yourself Jewish, of our brother Judah and you do not believe in Christ then let's hear what Christ has to say about that.

> 2 John 7 For many **deceivers** are entered into the world, who **confess not that Jesus Christ is come in the flesh. This is a deceiver and an antichrist**. KJV

> Rev 2:9 I know thy works, and tribulation, and poverty, (but thou art rich) and **I know the blasphemy of them which say they are Jews, and are not, but are the synagogue of Satan**. KJV

You see, another great deception that the antichrists would have us believe is that they, calling themselves Jews, and Blue Bloods are the chosen ones and we are Heathen or Gentiles. **WRONG!**

Good con job and they have gotten away with turning everything upside down because of our lack of knowledge. Shame on US!

Hos 4:1 Hear the word of the LORD, ye children of Israel: for the **LORD hath a controversy** with the inhabitants of the land, because **there is no truth, nor mercy, nor knowledge of God** in the land. KJV

The Blessed Nation under God is of the 10 scattered tribes of Israel. Read America in the Bible and send for book by Raymond Capt called, "The Abrahamic Covenant".

If you are a Christian, Passover is the highest Holy Day of Christianity where we take Communion with Christ, being covered with His blood, repenting and receiving forgiveness of our sins and passed over by the death angel as it was in Egypt, (which means bondage), when God brought us out with HIS mighty hand.

If they only knew where the Ten (10) lost tribes of Israel are, then they would realize that we in the good old USA are of Israel, under the Covenant God made with Abraham (the father of many Nations) and a Christian Nation. Please read the Abrahamic Covenant that God made concerning the house of Israel and the house of Judah our brother, all 12 tribes.

Let us look at Easter and Passover as found in the Old and the New

117

Testament. We will then look at the traditions of men which seek to change the times (Daniel 7: 25) and make the Word of God void and of none effect.

New Testament: 1 Cor 5:7 Purge out therefore the old leaven, that ye may be a new lump, as ye are unleavened. For even **Christ our passover is sacrificed for us**:

What is the special sacrifice and where did this originate?

Ex 12:11-13
11 And thus shall ye eat it; with your loins girded, your shoes on your feet, and your staff in your hand; and ye shall eat it in haste: it is the LORD's passover.

12 For I will pass through the land of Egypt this night, and will smite all the firstborn in the land of Egypt, both man and beast; and against all the gods of Egypt I will execute judgment: I am the LORD. 13 **And the blood shall be to you for a token upon the houses where ye are: and when I see the blood, I will pass over you, and the plague shall not be upon you to destroy you, when I smite the land of Egypt.**

Does the Passover apply to Christians today? Yes! Christ is our Passover. This means that we should eat the

Passover Lamb (Eat the word of God).

1 Cor 5:7 Purge out therefore
the old leaven, that ye may be
a new lump, as ye are
unleavened. **For even Christ our
passover is sacrificed for us**:

John 1:1:1 In the beginning was
the Word, and the Word was with
God, and the Word was God.
John 1:14 And the Word was made
flesh, and dwelt among us, (and
we beheld his glory, the glory
as of the only begotten of the
Father,) full of grace and
truth.

How do we eat the word of God? As it
is written, the Word was God and the
Word was made flesh. We should eat the
Word of God and we should eat the
Passover Lamb.

John 6:53-56
53 Then Jesus said unto them,
Verily, verily, I say unto you,
Except ye eat the flesh of the
Son of man, and drink his
blood, ye have no life in you.
54 **Whoso eateth my flesh, and
drinketh my blood, hath eternal
life; and I will raise him up
at the last day.**
55 For my flesh is meat indeed,
and my blood is drink indeed.56
He that eateth my flesh, and
drinketh my blood, dwelleth in
me, and I in him.

This is why we have communion as Jesus

Christ as was performed at the last supper before He was crucified. There is a two fold purpose for doing this; first, eating the Passover meal (Communion) is a token of the actual eating of the Lamb in Exodus and secondly, the blood then is placed over our door posts (where we tabernacle),where we shall be passed over by the plagues and destruction. We must also eat the Word (God's words as in read the Book).

Let us look at what the Holy Spirit reveals to us about this from Revelations.

> Rev 7:14 And I said unto him, Sir, thou knowest. And he said to me, These are they which came out of great tribulation, and have washed their robes, and made them white in the **blood of the Lamb.**

> 1 Peter 1:18 Forasmuch as ye know that ye were not redeemed with corruptible things, as silver and gold, from your vain conversation received by tradition from your fathers; 19 But with the precious blood of Christ, as of a lamb without blemish and without spot:

How and where did the Easter tradition come from and how did it work it's way into our churches? For openers, Easter is only mentioned once in the bible and it is improperly translated from the manuscripts. Let's look.

Acts 12:4 And when he had apprehended him, he put him in prison, and delivered him to four quaternions of soldiers to keep him; intending after <u>Easter</u> to bring him forth to the people.
5 Peter therefore was kept in prison: but prayer was made without ceasing of the church unto God for him.

Easter in the Greek as used in this verse: NT:3957 **pascha (pas'-khah)**; of Aramaic origin [compare OT:6453]; the <u>Passover</u> (the meal, the day, the festival or the special sacrifices connected with it): KJV - Easter, Passover. Let us look up Passover in the Greek.

Passover: NT:3957 pascha (pas'-khah); of Aramaic origin [compare OT:6453]; the Passover (the meal, the day, the festival or the special sacrifices connected with it):

Now we know that even the one time we see the word Easter in KJV Bible that it was a mistranslation from the word "pascha" which means, "the Passover meal, day,, the festival".

Now, let us find out what EASTER really means, who promoted this idea and where this tradition stems from and worked it's way into our churches.

The real word EASTRE and not the mistranslation of pascah or Passover back to Easter.

Easter: From the Greek word Ishtar and Ashtaroth which was: ASHTAROTH [ASH tah rahth] (wives) - the plural form of Ashtoreth, a pagan goddess. 1 Sam 31:10 connects her with the Philistines, and 1 Kings 11:5 connects her with the Sidonians. She was often considered the companion or partner of the male god BAAL (Judg 2:13).(from Nelson's Illustrated Bible Dictionary, Copyright (c)1986, Thomas Nelson Publishers)

ASHTAROTH
Apparently the worship of these goddesses was practiced by the Israelites from time to time. Solomon compromised his faith by worshiping at the altar of Ashtaroth (1 Kings 11:5,33). Along with the Baalim (the plural of Baal), the Ashtaroth were thought by the Philistines to be responsible for fertility and the growth of crops and herds.

The Ashtaroth were worshiped by other peoples under such names as Astarte (Phoenicians and Canaanites), Inanna (Sumerians), Ishtar (Babylonians), Aphrodite (Greeks), and Venus (Romans). All these were goddesses of sensual love and fertility.
(from Nelson's Illustrated Bible Dictionary, Copyright (c)1986, Thomas Nelson Publishers)

The proof that this is false and has worked it's way into our traditions is *the Easter bunny, representing the goddess of sex and fertility, thus the Easter egg. Lets play hide the egg.*

We actually have become so ignorant that we allow this type of tradition to be taught to our children.

For the deeper study check this out:

ASHTAROTH, CITY OF ASHTAROTH ASH'TAROTH (ash'ta-roth).

1. An ancient city of Bashan, E of the Jordan (Deut 1:4; Josh 9:10; 12:4; 13:12,31) in the half tribe of Manasseh. The inhabitants, including King Og, were giants. The town was the seat of the lewd worship of Astarte and was the capital of Og. By the time of Israel's entrance into the land, the iniquity of the inhabitants was full (Gen 15:16), and God commanded the conquering Israelites to utterly exterminate them (Deut 3:2-6). The site of the ancient city is identified with Tell Ashtarab, twenty-one miles E of the Sea of Galilee, the hill being surrounded by a well-watered plain.
2. The plural form of the god Ashtoreth (Astarte). See Gods, False. (from The New Unger's Bible Dictionary. Originally published by Moody Press of Chicago, Illinois. Copyright (c) 1988.)

GODS, FALSE Ashtoreth (Astarte) and Anath. Frequently represented as a nude woman bestride a lion, with a lily in one hand and a serpent in the other, and called Qudshu "the Holiness," that is, "the Holy One" in a perverted moral

sense, she was a divine courtesan. In the same sense the male prostitutes consecrated to the cult of the Qudshu and prostituting themselves to her honor were called qedeshim, "sodomites" (Deut 23:18, marg.; 1 Kings 14:24; 15:12; 22:46). Characteristically Canaanite, the lily symbolizes grace and sex appeal and the serpent fertility (W. F. Albright, Archaeology and the Religion of Israel [1942], pp. 68-94). At Byblos (biblical Gebal) on the Mediterranean, N of Sidon, a center dedicated to this goddess has been excavated. She and her colleagues specialized in sex and war, and her shrines were temples of legalized vice.
(from The New Unger's Bible Dictionary. Originally published by Moody Press of Chicago, Illinois. Copyright (c) 1988.)

If we go back to the study of the Fallen angels and Giants we see that the offspring of the fallen angels were giants. OG king of Bashan was one of these giants or children of the fallen ones. So now **we see who and where this originated.**

There is nothing new under the sun. We stood by and watched as the offspring of Cain, who had all intermingled with one another as well as intermingled with the fallen ones yelled; "Crucify Him" and let their brother "Barabbas" go.
Who was the first murderer?
Cain, Yes. Now we know why they (Cain's offspring) screamed to let their brother, Barabbas the murderer go. Look around you today and see. We have

children murdering for fun. We also know
that our LORD has a perfect plan of
saving His children from the Evil ones.

First we need to seek and know the
TRUTH.

BARABBAS
[buh RAB bas] (son of Abbas) - a
"robber" (John 18:40) and "notorious
prisoner" (Matt 27:16) who was chosen
by the mob in Jerusalem to be <u>released
instead of Jesus. Barabbas had been
imprisoned for insurrection and murder</u>
(Luke 23:19,25; Mark 15:7). Pilate
offered to give the crowd either Jesus
or Barabbas. The mob demanded that he
release Barabbas and crucify Jesus.
There is no further mention of
Barabbas after he was released. (from
Nelson's Illustrated Bible Dictionary,
Copyright (c)1986, Thomas Nelson
Publishers)

What is the first commandment?

Ex 20:3 Thou shalt have no
other gods before me. KJV

What else?

Ex 20:7
7 Thou shalt not take the name
of the LORD thy God in vain;
<u>for the LORD will not hold him
guiltless that taketh his name
in vain.</u> KJV

This means that we shall not teach nor
make the LORD'S name empty or vain by
traditions of men that pervert God's

125

words and make it of none effect and void. What did God just say about those who do this?

> 1 Sam 12:21 And turn ye not aside: for then should ye go after **vain things, which cannot profit nor deliver; for they are vain (empty).**

> Deut 4:29-31 But if from thence thou shalt seek the LORD thy God, thou shalt find him, **if** thou seek him with all thy heart and with all thy soul.

> Deut. 30 **When thou art in tribulation, and all these things are** come upon thee, **even in the latter days,** **if** thou turn to the LORD thy God, and shalt be obedient unto his voice;

> 31(For the LORD thy God is a merciful God;) he will not forsake thee, neither destroy thee, nor forget the covenant of thy fathers which he sware unto them. KJV

Chapter X

God is a Divorcee

The next time anyone tries to put you
in bondage or on a guilt trip because
you are divorced, feel free to tell
them to start with God first.
Divorce is always painful for both
parties and not a good thing it even
happened to our GOD.

> Jer 3:6-8
> 6 The LORD said also unto me in
> the days of Josiah the king, Hast
> thou seen that which backsliding
> Israel hath done? she is gone up
> upon every high mountain and
> under every green tree, and there
> hath played the harlot.
> 7 And I said after she had done
> all these things, Turn thou unto
> me. But she returned not. And her
> treacherous sister Judah saw it.
> 8 And I saw, when for all the
> causes whereby backsliding <u>Israel</u>
> <u>committed adultery **I had put her**</u>
> **<u>away, and given her a bill of</u>**
> **<u>divorce</u>**; yet her treacherous
> sister Judah feared not, but went
> and played the harlot also.

God forgives our sins. If you have had
to divorce or deviate from
righteousness; pray, asking forgiveness
and repent (have a change of heart)
thereby trying to do that which is
right, just and true. Upon repentance
and by forgiveness through the blood of
Christ you are forgiven and cleansed.
Period! End of story. God never wants

to hear about it again.

Worship God, as only He can save through Yeshua, Jesus Christ.

> Mark 3:28 Verily I say unto you, **All sins shall be forgiven unto the sons of men**, and blasphemies wherewith soever they shall blaspheme: 29 But he that shall blaspheme against the Holy Ghost hath never forgiveness, but is in danger of eternal damnation:

The only time that the unforgivable sin may be committed is when God's witnesses or Elect are delivered up before the Antichrist. If they deny the Holy Spirit of the LORD to speak through them. At that time and only then may this sin be done. I personally do not think it is possible that this will happen to anyone who is chosen to be delivered up. God does the choosing and He is in total control.

> Mark 13:11
> 11 But when they shall lead you, and deliver you up, take no thought beforehand what ye shall speak, neither do ye premeditate: but whatsoever shall be given you in that hour, that speak ye: for it is not ye that speak, but the Holy Ghost.
> KJV

Chapter XI

Is there such a thing as reincarnation?

Here is what is written about how many times man in the flesh must die.

Heb 9:27 And as it is appointed unto men **once to die,** but after this the judgment: KJV

Here is a second witness to this.

Eccl 9:5-6 For the living know that they shall die: but the dead know not any thing, neither have they any more a reward; for the memory of them is forgotten. 6 Also their love, and their hatred, and their envy, is now perished; neither have they any more a portion **for ever** in any thing that is done under the sun. KJV

Here is a third witness and the words of Jesus as he tried to explain this to Nocodemus who was a Very knowledgeable man in the scriptures and possessed much common sense.

John 3:1-8 There was a man of the Pharisees, named Nicodemus, a ruler of the Jews: 2 The same came to Jesus by night, and said unto him, Rabbi, we know that thou art a teacher

come from God: for no man
can do these miracles that
thou doest, except God be
with him. 3 Jesus answered
and said unto him,

Verily, verily, I say unto
thee, Except a man be born
again, he cannot see the
kingdom of God. 4 Nicodemus
saith unto him, How can a man
be born when he is old? can he
enter the second time into his
mother's womb, and be born?

What does Jesus mean, "born again"?
Let us look up the Greek translation
of the words born again.

Be Born: NT:1080 gennao (ghen-nah'-o);
from a variation of NT:1085; to
procreate (properly, of the father,
but by extension of the mother);
figuratively, **to regenerate**:

Again: NT:509 anothen (an'-o-then);
from NT:507; from above; by analogy,
from the first; by implication, **anew**:

How could a man be regenerated anew?
Let's let Jesus explain this.

5 Jesus answered, Verily,
verily, I say unto thee, Except
a man be born of water and of
the Spirit, he cannot enter
into the kingdom of God.

Water and spirit is referring to the water of the womb (one must be born into this flesh Earth Age) at child birth and the spirit which returns to the Father at death.

We are instructed to use Baptism as a symbol to God of our dying to things of the flesh, receiving the Holy Spirit as Jesus also did and Jesus' resurrection (regeneration anew) in the spirit with the Father now and upon the death of the flesh.

6 That which is born of the flesh is flesh; and that which is born of the Spirit is spirit.

7 Marvel not that I said unto thee, Ye must be born again.

Jesus is explaining what happens to our spirit when we return to the Father at the death of the flesh. You can feel the wind, you can hear it, you know it is there but you can not see it, or possess it, or can it , imprison it. or hold it in your hand.

8 The **wind** bloweth where it listeth, and thou hearest the sound thereof, but canst not tell whence it cometh, and whither it goeth: so is every one that is born of the **Spirit.** KJV

Now we shall get to the meaning of the word "Wind" in Greek as used in the New Testament.

Wind: NT:4151 pneuma (pnyoo'-mah); from NT:4154; a current of air, i.e. breath (blast) or a breeze; by analogy or figuratively, a spirit, i.e. (human) the rational soul, (by implication) vital principle, mental disposition, etc., or (superhuman) an angel, demon, or (divine) God, Christ's spirit, the Holy Spirit:

Here we see that it is explained further by Jesus.

> 1 Cor 15:50-54 Now this I say, brethren, that **flesh and blood cannot inherit the kingdom of God**; neither doth corruption inherit incorruption.

No way! If you think you are going to come up out of your grave you very well might, but not into the Kingdom of God. Whose kingdom then?

> 51 **Behold, I shew you a mystery**; We shall not all sleep, but we shall all be changed, 52 In a moment, in the twinkling of an eye, at the last trump: for the trumpet shall sound(#7 trumpet), and the dead (dead in Christ to the worldly flesh) shall be raised incorruptible (Into that Spirit body), and we shall be changed.

53 For this corruptible (man) must put on incorruption (his spiritual body), and this mortal must put on immortality (deathlessness).
54 So when this corruptible shall have put on incorruption, and this mortal shall have put on immortality, then shall be brought to pass the saying that is written, <u>Death is swallowed up in victory</u>. KJV

Here is the beginning and end of the matter.

Gen 3:19 In the sweat of thy face shalt thou eat bread, <u>**till thou return unto the ground; for out of it wast thou taken: for dust thou art, and unto dust shalt thou return**</u>. KJV

Eccl 12:7 Then shall the dust return to the earth as it was: and the spirit shall return unto God who gave it. KJV

Chapter XII

Sins of the Fathers carried over to the children. NOT SO!

Let us look at God's Word where man has taken this from.

This is where some preachers and teachers come up with the idea that sins of fathers are passed on to their sons.

> Deut 5:9-10 Thou shalt not bow down thyself unto them, nor serve them: (Them, is false gods, graven images and lies that go contrary to God's word) for I the LORD thy God am a jealous God, visiting the iniquity of the fathers upon the children unto the third and fourth generation **of them that hate me**,
> 10 And shewing mercy unto thousands of them that love me and keep my commandments.

Guess those teachers must have left out the, "of those that hate me", so if you love the Lord, keep His commandments and believe in Jesus Christ, then you do not fall into this category no matter what your fathers have done. Jesus came to set us free by repentance and His Mercy of forgiveness.

Let's look further.

Jer 31:29-30 In those days <u>they</u> <u>shall say no more</u>, The fathers have eaten a sour grape, and the children's teeth are set on edge. 30 But **every one shall die for his own iniquity**: every man that eateth the sour grape, his teeth shall be set on edge.

Ever hear our expression, "He ate Sour Grapes"?

Looking further for a third witness.

Ezek 18:20-22
20 The **soul** that sinneth, it **shall die**. **The son shall not bear the iniquity of the father,** neither shall the father bear the iniquity of the son: the righteousness of the righteous shall be upon him, and the wickedness of the wicked shall be upon him. 21 But **if** the wicked will turn from all his sins that he hath committed, and keep all my statutes, and do that which is lawful and right, he shall surely live, he shall not die. 22 All his transgressions that he hath committed, they shall not be mentioned unto him: in his righteousness that he hath done he shall live.

This about sums up the Justice and fairness of God.

Gal 6:7-8 Be not deceived; God is not mocked: for **whatsoever a man soweth, that shall he also reap.**
8 **For he that soweth to his flesh shall of the flesh reap corruption; but he that soweth to the Spirit shall of the Spirit reap life everlasting.**

Chapter XIII

What is Deception?
What is sin and
What happens when we repent?

Taking a close look at deception.
Do you remember when you believed in
Santa Clause? Most of us could figure
out that a fat man couldn't fit down a
small chimney and to make matters
worse, it didn't seem possible that
this man could visit all children on
the face of the Earth in one night and
carry that many gifts in a sack. What
did we do? We allowed our own
imaginations to fill in the illogical
blanks so that we could believe
something that was not in reality
believable. Why? Because we liked the
blessings or gifts that were promised
if we believed.

How did you feel when you learned that
the closest people to you whom you
trusted totally had deceived you?

We are going to take our vain
imaginations out of the loop and let the
Word of God speak in truth.

In order to know what sin really is and
what the consequences of committing sin
are, we should first learn the meaning
of sin..

What is sin according to Strongs.

Hebrew word SIN: OT:2398 chata' (khaw-taw'); a primitive root; properly, **to miss**; hence (figuratively and generally) to sin; by inference, to forfeit, lack, expiate, repent, (causatively) **lead astray**, condemn:

We need to learn the LORD'S methods and how much He really loves His children, you and me.

After this we will begin to see His way of doing things which are called Truth and righteousness.

In the flesh we are incapable of being good or righteous; however, God in His love has also **provided a way** for us to overcome all of our faults and He promises that He will never forsake us or leave us as long as we are trying to do what is just and right according to HIM not man.

The more we learn about God by His living word, the more we come to know Him and how He does things. This brings great respect as we see His wonderful works and we begin to love Him and as our love grows we want to do things that please Him. We want to emulate our Father and be just like Him.

> Matt 9:12-13
> 12 But when Jesus heard that, he said unto them, They that be whole need not a physician, but they that are sick. **13 But go ye and**

learn what that meaneth, <u>I</u>
<u>will have mercy, and not</u>
<u>sacrifice</u>: for I am not
come to call the righteous,
but sinners to repentance.

What does Mercy mean?

Mercy:NT:1656 eleos (el'-eh-os); of
uncertain affinity; <u>compassion</u> (human
or divine, especially active):

Sacrifice:NT:2380 thuo (thoo'-o); a
primary verb; properly, to rush
(breathe hard, **blow, smoke**), i.e. (by
implication) to sacrifice (properly, by
fire, but genitive case); by extension
to immolate **(slaughter for any**
purpose):

Blowing smoke seems to be what we are
seeing all around us if our eyes are
open.

Is anyone blowing smoke that you know
of? Like, "You're going to burn in Hell
if you don't do this and you don't do
that." Not so! The lake of fire only
happens at the end of the millenium to
those who by free will who; after
seeing the marvelous works of the LORD
and HIS great mercy still hate HIM and
continue to follow Satan's unrighteous
unclean and unholy teachings.

Did you know that causing God's
children to walk through the fire as
in, you are going to burn in Hell if
you don't do this or that. In fact that
teaching is totally contrary to the
freedom that our Father promises HIS

children. This teaching puts God's children into bondage instead of freedom. This is why Christ says:

> John 8:32 And ye shall know the truth, and the truth shall make you free.

Now looking into what God says about causing HIS children to walk through the fire, like you're going to Hell. NOT SO !!

> Ezek 16:20-24 **Moreover thou hast taken thy sons and thy daughters,** whom thou hast borne unto me, and these hast thou sacrificed unto them to be devoured. **Is this of thy whoredoms a small matter,**
>
> 21 **That thou hast slain my children, and delivered them to cause them to pass through the fire for them**?

Like telling them they will go to HELL if they don't follow <u>their</u> doctrines.

> 22 And in all thine abominations and thy whoredoms thou hast not remembered the days of thy youth, when thou wast naked and bare, and wast polluted in thy blood. 23 And it came to pass after all thy wickedness, (woe, woe unto thee! saith the Lord GOD;)

Who is the Lord GOD talking to?

24 That thou hast also built unto thee an eminent place, and hast made thee an high place in every street. KJV

Do you see the churches?

There has been only one; the son of perdition, who has been sentenced to perish and that one is Satan.

What may we say?

Do things the easy way or do them the hard way during the millenium

What does Trespasses mean?

Trespass:NT:3900 paraptoma (par-ap'-to-mah); from NT:3895; **a side-slip (lapse or deviation)**, i.e. (unintentional) error or (wilful) transgression:NT:3895 parapipto (par-ap-ip'-to); from NT:3844 and NT:4098; to **fall aside**, i.e. (figuratively) to **apostatize**:

Let us take a look at what apostasy means.

APOSTASY: nature of apostasy is shown by such passages as Heb 10:26-29; 2 Peter 2:15-21, and John 15:22. Apostasy as **the act of a professed Christian, who knowingly and deliberately rejects revealed truth regarding the deity of Christ (1 John 4:1-3) and redemption through His atoning sacrifice** (Phil

3:18; 2 Peter 2:1) (from The New
Unger's Bible Dictionary. Originally
published by Moody Press of
Chicago,Illinois.copyright(c)1988.)

**APOSTASY; APOSTATE (a-pos'-ta-si), (a-
pos'-tat) (he apostasia, "a standing
away from"): I.e. <u>a falling away, a
withdrawal, a defection</u>**

> 2 Peter 3:5-6 <u>**For this they
> willingly are ignorant**</u> of, that
> by the word of God the heavens
> were of old, and the earth
> standing out of the water and
> in the water: 6 Whereby the
> world that then was, being
> overflowed with water,
> perished:

**Willingly ignorant of what is seen by us
in the Earth today, like the extinction
and destruction of the earth that was
along with the Dinosaurs.**

**You can plant a seed in the ground,
water it and grunt over it forever. It
is God and only He makes the seed grow.**

God came here to this Earth in the
flesh to make a way for us to
reconsider, repent(change our minds)
and return to Him and he promises that
if we do this He will return to us.

> 2 Cor 5:18-19 And all
> things are of God, who hath
> reconciled us to himself by
> Jesus Christ, and hath
> given to us the ministry of
> reconciliation;19 To wit,

that God was in Christ,
reconciling the world unto
himself, **not imputing their
trespasses unto them;** and
hath committed unto us the
word of reconciliation.

What does God want us to do?

Mic 6:8 He hath shewed
thee, O man, what is good;
and what doth the LORD
require of thee, but to **do
justly, and to love mercy,
and to walk humbly with thy
God?**

Humbly: OT:6800 tsana` (tsaw-nah'); a
primitive root; to humiliate:

John 3:17-18
**17 For God sent not his Son
into the world to condemn the
world; but that the world
through him might be saved.
18 He that believeth on him
is not condemned:** but he that
believeth not is condemned
already, because he hath not
believed in the name of the
only begotten Son of God.

IF Jesus doesn't condemn us who
does man think he is that he would
condemn us? Who is the accuser?
Yes, the accuser is Satan and his
Ministers disguised as ministers of
righteousness.

2 Cor 11:14-15 And no marvel;
for Satan himself is

transformed (G-3345 disguised)into an angel of light. 15 Therefore it is no great thing if his ministers also be transformed (G-3345 disguised) as the ministers of righteousness; whose end shall be according to their works. KJV

John 5:22 For the Father judgeth no man, but hath committed all judgment unto the Son:

John 5:23-24 That all men should honour the Son, even as they honour the Father. He that honoureth not the Son honoureth not the Father which hath sent him.

24 Verily, verily, I say unto you, He that heareth my word, and believeth on him that sent me, hath everlasting life, and shall not come into condemnation; but is passed from death unto life.

John 6:33 For the bread of God is he which cometh down from heaven, and giveth life unto the world. John 8:27-32 They understood not that he spake to them of the Father.
28 Then said Jesus unto them, When ye have lifted up the Son of man, then shall ye know that I am he, and that I do nothing of myself; but as my

Father hath taught me, I speak
these things. 29 And he that
sent me is with me: the Father
hath not left me alone; **for I
do always those things that
please him.** 30 As he spake
these words, many believed on
him. 31 Then **said Jesus to
those Jews which believed on
him, If ye continue in my
word, then are ye my disciples
indeed; 32 And ye shall know
the truth, and the truth shall
make you free.**

John 8:36
36 If the Son therefore shall
make you free, ye shall be
free indeed.

Free: NT:1659 eleutheroo (el-yoo-ther-
o'-o); from NT:1658; to **liberate**, i.e.
(figuratively) to exempt (from moral,
ceremonial or mortal liability):

John 8:51 Verily, verily, I say
unto you, If a man keep my
saying, he shall never see death:

Let us now learn what repentance is:

Repentance: NT:3341 metanoia (met-an'-
oy-ah); from NT:3340; (subjectively)
compunction (for guilt, including
reformation); by implication reversal
(of [another's] decision): **NT:3340
metanoeo (met-an-o-eh'-o); from NT:3326
and NT:3539; to think differently or
afterwards, i.e. reconsider (morally,
feel compunction):**

145

One must begin by repenting (reconsider or think differently) about his own ways and consider God's ways which always remain constant and true. Ask for forgiveness of our trespasses (falling away from that which is just and compassionate). God's laws never change and are always the same.

Example: One of God's laws is Gravity. We all know that God's laws do not change and always work the same.
The sun always rises in the East and sets in the West.
A cow has always been a cow and will always be a cow.
A duck is a duck and will always be a duck.
North, East, South and West shall always be the same.

All of God's sayings and truths (Precepts) are the same yesterday, today and tomorrow. So do not let anyone blow smoke at you trying to give you another truth that God has not said.

When we repent (reconsider or begin to think differently) this is what our Father says He will do by Jesus Christ.

> **Mal 3:6-7 6 For I am the LORD, I change not; therefore ye sons of Jacob are not consumed. 7 Even from the days of your fathers ye are gone away from mine ordinances, and have not kept them.** Return unto me, and I will return unto you, saith the LORD of hosts. **But ye said, Wherein shall we return?**

> Luke 17:3-4 <u>Take heed to
> yourselves: If thy brother
> trespass against thee, rebuke
> him; and if he repent, forgive
> him.</u> 4 And if he trespass
> against thee seven times in a
> day, and seven times in a day
> turn again to thee, saying, I
> repent; thou shalt forgive him.

See, God would not ask us to do
anything he wouldn't do himself. As
God's children and we all are, like it
or not. God came in the flesh as our
King and High Priest delivering His
word and His love, asking us to repent
(reconsider) and try His ways which
lead to blessings, peace, freedom,
eternal life and happiness.

> Heb 13:5 Let your
> conversation be without
> covetousness; (greediness)
> and be content with such
> things as ye have: for he
> hath said, I will never
> leave thee, nor forsake
> thee.

Are you Deceived?

Luke 21:8 Jesus' words: 8 And he said, Take heed that ye **be not deceived**: for **many shall come in my name, saying, I am Christ**; and the time draweth near: **go ye not therefore after them**.

In Christ's name means calling themselves Christians.

Deceive: NT:4105 planao (plan-ah'-o); from NT:4106; **to (properly, cause to) roam (from safety, truth, or virtue):**

Matt 24:4-5 And Jesus answered and said unto them, **Take heed that no man deceive you.** 5 For many shall come in my name, saying, I am Christ;= Christians and **shall deceive many**.

2 Thess 2:3-4 **Let no man deceive you by any means**: for that day shall not come, except there come a **falling away first**, (APOSTASY: A falling away from the faith) and that **man of sin be revealed, the son of perdition**; (only son of God sentenced to perish and one of satan's names, Apollyon).

2 Thes.4 Who opposeth and exalteth himself above all that is called God, or that is worshipped; so that he as God

sitteth in the temple (in Jerusalem) of God, shewing himself that he is God.

This is Satan deceiving you if you are not standing on the ROCK of TRUTH.

2 Thess 2:10-12 And with all deceivableness of unrighteousness in them that perish; because they received not the love of the truth, that they might be saved. 11 And for this cause **God shall send them** strong delusion, that they should believe a lie.

Why would God be sending the strong delusion, Satan?

Because they loved not hearing the words of God which are TRUTH. Instead they would hear fables and traditions that make void the word of God.

2 Tim 4:3-4 For the time will come when they will not endure sound doctrine; but after their own lusts shall they heap to themselves teachers, having itching ears;4 And they shall turn away their ears from the truth, and shall be turned unto fables. KJV

This is when God's wrath boils over and He tells Michael to let Satan have at us.

149

12 That they all might be damned who believed not the truth, but had pleasure in unrighteousness

Deut 11:16-21 Take heed to yourselves, that your heart be not deceived, and ye turn aside, and serve other gods, and worship them;17 And then the LORD's wrath be kindled against you, and he shut up the heaven, that there be no rain, and that the land yield not her fruit; and lest ye perish quickly from off the good land which the LORD giveth you. **18 Therefore shall ye lay up these my words in your heart and in your soul, and bind them for a sign upon your hand, that they may be as frontlets between your eyes.19 And ye shall teach them your children, speaking of them when thou sittest in thine house, and when thou walkest by the way, when thou liest down, and when thou risest up.**20 And thou shalt write them upon the door posts of thine house, and upon thy gates:21 That your days may be multiplied, and the days of your children, in the land which the LORD sware unto

your fathers to give them,
as the days of heaven upon
the earth.

We are commanded to KEEP GOD'S WORDS.

1 Cor 15:33-36 **Be not
deceived**: evil
communications corrupt good
manners. 34 Awake to
righteousness, and sin not;
for some have not the
knowledge of God: I speak
this to your shame.

35 But some man will say,
How are the dead raised up?
and with what body do they
come? 36 Thou fool, that
which thou sowest is not
quickened, except it die:

Gal 6:7-8 **Be not deceived**;
God is not mocked: for
whatsoever a man soweth,
that shall he also reap.
8 For he that soweth to his
flesh shall of the flesh
reap corruption; but he
that soweth to the Spirit
shall of the Spirit reap
life everlasting.

Titus 3:3-5 For we
ourselves also were
sometimes foolish,
disobedient, **deceived**,
serving divers lusts and
pleasures, living in malice
and envy, hateful, and
hating one another.4 But

151

after that the kindness and
love of God our Saviour
toward man appeared,5 Not
by works of righteousness
which we have done, but
**according to his mercy he
saved us**, by the washing of
regeneration, and renewing
of the Holy Ghost;

By HIS Grace are we saved and not by our
own works which are evil in the flesh.

THOUGHT FOR YOU:

**Every thought you have, where does it
come from?**

Where did it begin?

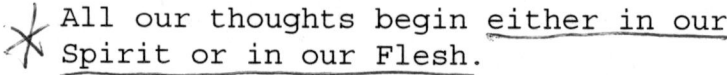

All our thoughts begin either in our
Spirit or in our Flesh.

If we walk in our spirit we are nothing.
Now, if we walk in TRUTH and the Holy
Spirit of the LORD we find everlasting
life, HIS blessings and PEACE.

BEWARE! There are also evil Spirits that
would have us think with our flesh minds
that they are Holy and lead us into
darkness and deception.

How do we tell the difference?

Know the Holy Word of God (not mans
traditions or man's words) and Keep it
with us as Jesus instructs.

If, we walk in the flesh we are no
better than a brute beast serving the

flesh which is feeble, lustful, sickly and weak.

Now let's see what is going to become of Babylon, the great confusion of the end times.

> Rev 18:21 Thus with violence shall that great city **Babylon (confusion and tyranny N-897)** be thrown down, and shall be found no more at all. Rev 18:23 And the light of a candle shall shine no more at all in thee; and the voice of the bridegroom and of the bride shall be heard no more at all in thee: for thy merchants were the great men of the earth; **for by thy sorceries were all nations deceived.**

Sorceries: NT:5331 pharmakeia (far-mak-i'-ah); from NT:5332; medication ("pharmacy"), i.e. (by extension) magic (literally or figuratively): **KJV - sorcery, witchcraft.**

> Rev: 18: 24 And in her (Babylon) was found the blood of prophets, and of saints, and of all that were slain upon the earth.

> Rev 19:20 And the beast was taken, and with him the **false prophet** that wrought miracles before him, with which he

deceived **them that had received the mark of the beast, and them that worshipped his image.** These both were cast alive into a lake of fire burning with brimstone.

Beast: NT:2339 thera (thay'-rah); from ther (a wild animal, as game); hunting, i.e. (figuratively) **destruction: - trap**.

False Prophet:
NT:5578 pseudoprophetes (psyoo-dop-rof-ay'-tace); from NT:5571 and NT:4396; a spurious prophet, i.e. **pretended foreteller or religious impostor:**
NT:5574 pseudomai (psyoo'-dom-ahee); middle voice of an apparently primary verb; to **utter an untruth or attempt to deceive by falsehood:**

You should have a good idea of what deception is and what the greater sin is; that of worshiping that which is false, untrue, disguised as righteous, failing to keep God's words of truth and righteousness within you.

You see, every thought that one has stems from that spirit living within him. Every action is the result of the growth of that which is planted within. Some good and some evil. This is why we should keep that which is good, true, righteous, holy and of the Lord within us, and reject the false else we will perish.

What is strong Delusion?

2 Thess 2:11-12 **And for this cause God shall send them strong delusion, that they should believe a lie: 12 That they all** might be damned **who** believed not the truth, **but had** pleasure in unrighteousness.

Now look up some of words from the Greek and rightly divide the word of God.

Strong Delusion:
NT:4108 planos (plan'-os); of uncertain affinity; roving (as a tramp), i.e. (by implication) an **impostor or misleader**; KJV - **deceiver, seducing.**

Damned: NT:2919 krino (kree'-no); properly, to distinguish, i.e. decide (mentally or judicially); by implication, to try, **condemn, punish:**

Unrighteousness: NT:93 adikia (ad-ee-kee'-ah); from NT:94; (legal) **injustice** (properly, the quality, by implication, the act); morally, wrongfulness (of character, life or act):

Now let us divide the word for truth, i.e. **"And for this cause God shall send them strong delusion (a deceiver)** that they all might be damned (punished) who believed not the truth but had pleasure in unrighteousness (injustice, morally wrong, the imposter or false Christ).

Example: What lie? We're going to be raptured out of here before the tribulation. Jesus is coming to take us away into the air. OOPS! Yes, Jesus is coming at the 7th trumpet; however, Satan (the deceiver, imposter), calling himself Jesus is coming at the 6th trumpet. God is the same today yesterday and forever. Doesn't it make sense that God would show us how He does things by using the story of Joshua (whose name means same as Jesus) who marched around Jericho six days, whereby the priests blew the trumpet each day and on the seventh day all the priests blew the 7 trumpets, all the people shouted and the walls came tumbling down.

> 1 Thess 4:16 For **the Lord himself shall descend from heaven with a shout, with the voice of the archangel, and with the trump of God**: and the dead in Christ shall rise first. (be resurrected to eternal life status from liable to die. Rom. 6: 4).

> Rev 14:8 And **there followed another angel, saying, Babylon is fallen, is fallen**, that great city, because she made all nations drink of the wine of the wrath of her fornication. (with the false bridegroom, the false prophet, the false Christ).

Speaking of the dead, the (ones who are already with Christ) shall rise (stand up with Him when He comes at the 7th, the last trumpet) first. "1 Cor 15:51-52 51 Behold,

> **I shew you a mystery;** We shall not all sleep, but we shall all be changed, 52 In a moment, in the twinkling of an eye, at **the last trump**: for the trumpet shall sound, and the **dead shall be raised incorruptible,** and **we shall be changed.**"

Yes! We will be here during the tribulation, or why would God say, "Eph 6:11 Put on the whole armour of God, that ye **may be able to stand** against the wiles of the devil." We are warned over and over again that the false Christ is coming first and that we need to be prepared mentally and spiritually.

<u>**Disobedience is**</u>: Mark 7:13 Making the word of God of none effect through **your tradition**, which ye have delivered: and **many such like things do ye.**

Disobedient: NT:544 apeitheo (ap-i-theh'-o); from NT:545; **to disbelieve (wilfully and perversely):** NT:545 apeithes (ap-i-thace'); from NT:1 (as a negative particle) and NT:3982; **unpersuadable, i.e. contumacious:(very resistant to uthority:** flagrantly insubordinate or rebellious).

Luke 11:28 But he said, Yea rather, **blessed** are they that **hear** **the word of God**, **and** **keep** it.

Not the words , vain bablings of man or dreams made up in men's minds.

11 Peter 2:7-8 Unto you therefore which believe he is precious : but unto them which be **disobedient**, (having pleasure in injustice) the stone which the builders disallowed, the same is made the head of the corner, 8 And a **stone of** **stumbling**, and a **rock of** **offence**, even to them **which** **stumble at the word, being** **disobedient** : whereunto also they were appointed.

Rom 11:25-33 For I would not, brethren, that ye should be ignorant of this **mystery,** lest ye should be wise in your own conceits; that **blindness in part is** **happened to Israel, until** **the fullness of the** **Gentiles be come in.**

You see, it is part of God's plan that
some stumble at the word because they
are disobedient to the LORD'S
instructions and others are blinded
until the fullness of time and God opens
their eyes to the TRUTH. It is an
amazing plan where our Father will
separate, divide and correct HIS
children with complete Justice and
fairness to all. It is written.

Chapter XIV

The Serpent in the wilderness
Our medical symbol of today.

Num 21:6 And the LORD sent
<u>fiery serpents</u> among the
people, and <u>they bit</u> the
people; and much people of
Israel died.
Num 21:7 Therefore the
people came to Moses, and
said, <u>We have sinned,</u> for we
have <u>spoken against the</u>
<u>LORD, and against thee;</u> pray
unto the LORD, that he take
away the serpents from us.
And Moses prayed for the
people.

FIERY: OT:8314 saraph (saw-rawf'); from
OT:8313; burning, i.e. (figuratively)
poisonous (serpent); specifically, a
saraph or symbolical creature (from
their **copper color)**: OT:8313 saraph
(saw-raf'); a primitive root; to be
(causatively, **set) on fire:**

SERPENT: OT:5175 nachash (naw-
khawsh'); from OT:5172; a snake (from
its hiss): OT:5172 nachash (naw-
khash'); a primitive root; properly, **to**
hiss, i.e. <u>whisper a (magic) spell;</u>
generally, to prognosticate:(Prophesy)

THEY BIT: OT:5391 nashak (naw-shak'); a
primitive root; to **strike with a sting**
(as a serpent); figuratively, to
oppress with interest on a loan:

The (fiery serpents) set the people on fire (praise the Lord) by whispering magic spells and prognosticating (prophesying out of their own minds) and oppressed the people from every direction, usury being one type and you'll go to Hell if you don't do our traditions.

1 Cor 10:9-11 Neither let us tempt Christ, as some of them also tempted, and were destroyed of serpents.
10 Neither murmur ye, as some of them also murmured, and were destroyed of the destroyer.

Destroyer: One of Satan's names. NT:3644 olothreutes (ol-oth-ryoo-tace'); from NT:3645; a ruiner, i.e. (specifically) a venomous serpent: NT:3645 olothreuo (ol-oth-ryoo'-o); from NT:3639; to spoil, i.e. slay: NT:3639 olethros (ol'-eth-ros); from a primary ollumi (to destroy; a prolonged form); uin, i.e. death, punishment:

11 Now all these things happened unto them for ensamples: and they are written for our admonition, upon whom the ends of the world are come.

Eccl 10:11 Surely the serpent will bite without enchantment; and a babbler is no better.

161

John 3:14-15
14 And as Moses lifted up the
serpent in the wilderness,
even so must the Son of man
be lifted up:

15 That whosoever believeth
in him should not perish,
but have eternal life.

Chapter XV

The seal of the Living God

Did you know that God is going to seal His servants before the False Christ, the Anti Christ and Satan shows up?

Did you know that Satan also has a seal?

Let us take a look at what God's word has to say about this.

> **Rev 7:2-3** And I saw another angel ascending from the east, having the **seal of the living God**: and he cried with a loud voice to the four angels, to whom it was given to hurt the earth and the sea, 3 Saying, Hurt not the earth, neither the sea, nor the trees, till we have sealed the servants of our God in their foreheads.

How does this seal or mark of God come about?

> Ezek 9:4 And the LORD said unto him, Go through the midst of the city, through the midst of Jerusalem, and set a mark upon the foreheads of the men that sigh and that cry for all the abominations that be done in the midst thereof.

These are Gods children who sigh and cry
from watching all of the abominations,
the idolatry going on this very day
along with the false teachings and
mistranslations of God's Holy Word.

Abominations from Strongs Concordance;
Hebrew, OT:8441 tow` ebah (to-ay-baw');
or to` ebah (to-ay-baw'); feminine
active participle of OT:8581; properly,
something disgusting (morally), i.e. (as
noun) an abhorrence; **especially idolatry**
or an idol: Like; Easter bunnies,
Rapture or Babbling in confusion.

> Ezek 9:5 And to the others he
> said in mine hearing, Go ye
> after him through the city, and
> smite: let not your eye spare,
> neither have ye pity: 6 Slay
> utterly old and young, both
> maids, and little children, and
> women: but come not near any man
> upon whom is the mark; and **begin
> at my sanctuary**. Then they began
> at the ancient men which were
> before the house.

What is the seal of the living God and
how does it compare with the seal or
mark of the Beast, Satan that is?

> Rev 13:16 And he causeth all,
> both small and great, rich and
> poor, free and bond, to receive
> a mark in their right hand, or
> in their foreheads:17 And that
> no man might buy or sell, save
> he that had the **mark**, or the
> **name** of the beast, or the **number**
> of his name.

How would one receive the mark of the beast?

What do we usually use our right hand for? Let's see giving tithes, buying, selling, helping the wrong or false Christ and the system that the false one or his children have set up.

If you haven't studied God's word then you really do not know if you are already marked by Satan or not, do you?

How would we receive the mark in our forehead?

That is where our brain is, therefore, if we have been deceived into believing the lies or wrong teachings because we refused to search God's word and prove it for ourselves. We were too lazy and didn't love the LORD enough to truthfully find out who He really is. We took the easy way as we honor God with our mouth when our heart is far from Him. Oh, how our Father wishes we loved Him enough to learn about Him!!

Rev 9:4 And it was commanded them that they should not hurt the grass of the earth, neither any green thing, neither any tree; but **only those men which have not the seal of God in their foreheads.**

165

5 And to them it was given that they should not kill them, but that they should be tormented five months: and their torment was as the torment of a scorpion, when he striketh a man.

The seal of the Living God is to know the 7 seals of Revelations as given by Christ in; Mark 13, Luke 21, Matt.24 and by all of the prophets where God tells us of His plan of salvation through the use of Satan, the false Christ, Antichrist, Little Rock, Deceiver, Father of the lie….

The mark of the beast (Satan) is to be deceived and believe his lies like; you won't be here during the tribulation.

The wrath or chastisement of God is His use of the Antichrist in demonstrating the depths of deception His children have allowed.

And then comes EXODUS, God's saving of His children through all of this.

Just the same way as He did from Egypt through Moses.

It is **very Important that we rightly divide the Word of God**. That we learn to break back the words to their original meanings for clarity as we are instructed by Christ to do.

There is another reason for this. In the original 1611 Bible Translation there was a letter in the front that explained that they were translating the Manuscripts against the will of the Church. Doesn't that sound about right?

We will add a couple of clips from the original pages. If you would like a copy of the entire writing that should come with each Bible please go to Kings Chapel or Shepherd's Chapel as in the Acknowledgements.

A few clips from the ORIGINAL

1611 EDITION OF THE KING JAMES BIBLE.

Note: this has been removed from the Bible by the PUBLISHERS?

For, was there ever any projected, that savored any way of newness or renewing, but the same endured many a storm of gainsaying, or opposition?

"TRANSLATION NECESSARY
But how shall men meditate in that, which they cannot understand? How shall they understand that which is kept close in an unknown tongue? as it is written, "Except I know the power of the voice, I shall be to him that speaketh, a Barbarian, and he that speaketh, shall be a Barbarian to me."

"THE UNWILLINGNESS OF OUR CHIEF ADVERSARIES, THAT THE SCRIPTURES SHOULD BE DIVULGED IN THE MOTHER TONGUE, ETC.

Now the Church of Rome would seem at the length to bear a motherly affection towards her children, and to allow them the Scriptures in their mother tongue: but indeed it is a gift, not deserving to be called a gift, an unprofitable gift: [Sophecles] they must first get a License in writing before they may use them, and to get that, they must approve themselves to their Confessor, that is, to be such as are, if not frozen in the dregs, yet soured with the leaven of their superstition. Howbeit, it seemed too much to Clement the Eighth that there should be any License granted to have them in the vulgar tongue, and therefore he overruleth and frustrateth the grant of Pius the Fourth.
So much are they afraid of the light of the Scripture, (Lucifugae Scripturarum, as Tertulian speaketh) that they will not trust the people with it, no not as it is set forth by their own sworn men, no not with the License of their own Bishops and Inquisitors. Yea, so unwilling they are to communicate the Scriptures to the people's understanding in any sort, that they are not ashamed to confess, that we forced them to translate it into English against their wills. This seemeth to argue a bad cause, or a bad conscience, or both. Sure we are, that it is not he that hath good gold, that is afraid to bring it to the touchstone, but he that hath the counterfeit; [Tertul. de resur. carnis.] neither is it the true man that shunneth

the light, but the malefactor, lest his deeds should be reproved [John 3:20]: neither is it the plain dealing Merchant that is unwilling to have the weights, or the meteyard brought in place, but he that useth deceit. But we will let them alone for this fault, and return to translation."

AN ANSWER TO THE IMPUTATIONS OF OUR ADVERSARIES
Now to the latter we answer; that we do not deny, nay we affirm and avow, that the very meanest translation of the Bible in English, set forth by men of our profession, (for we have seen none of theirs of the whole Bible as yet) containeth the word of God, nay, is the word of God. As the King's speech, which he uttereth in Parliament, being translated into French, Dutch, Italian, and Latin, is still the King's speech, though it be not interpreted by every Translator with the like grace, nor peradventure so fitly for phrase, nor so expressly for sense, everywhere. For it is confessed, that things are to take their denomination of the greater part; and a natural man could say, Verum ubi multa nitent in carmine, non ego paucis offendor maculis, etc. [Horace.] A man may be counted a virtuous man, though he have made many slips in his life, (else, there were none virtuous, for in many things we offend all) [James 3:2] also a comely man and lovely, though he have some warts upon his hand, yea, not only freckles upon his face, but also scars. **No cause therefore why the word translated should be denied to be the word, or forbidden to be current,**

169

notwithstanding that some imperfections and blemishes may be noted in the setting forth of it. For whatever was perfect under the Sun, where Apostles or Apostolic men, that is, men endued with an extraordinary measure of God's spirit, and privileged with the privilege of infallibility, had not their hand?"

"And whereas they urge for their second defence of their vilifying and abusing of the English Bibles, or some pieces thereof, which they meet with, for that heretics (forsooth) were the Authors of the translations, (heretics they call us by the same right that they call themselves Catholics, both being wrong) we marvel what divinity taught them so."

"And in what sort did these assemble? In the trust of their own knowledge, or of their sharpness of wit, or deepness of judgment, as it were in an arm of flesh? At no hand. They trusted in him that hath the key of David, opening and no man shutting; they prayed to the Lord the Father of our Lord, to the effect that S. Augustine did; "O let thy Scriptures be my pure delight, let me not be deceived in them, neither let me deceive by them."

We have just read a few clips from the, "letter to the reader of the Original 1611 Edition of the King James"

It is a basic warning to the readers to rightly divide the WORD.

170

Let's go to the False Prophet.

The false prophet spirit is the false Christ calling himself Christ and God, working miracles in the sight of men and giving you anything that you want (Rev.13 14) IF you will worship him and his beast system of peace, freedom and entitlement programs for all which is a lie. It comes with a price. Satan always has a price.

He wants your soul. Wait for our true Bridegroom to get here.

Now we are going to go through the 7 seals. The reason for this is so that we may possess the Keys of David, put the key into the lock and unseal the Book.

> John 3:33 He that hath received his testimony hath set to his seal that God is true. KJV

Pay particular attention to the 7th seal when Christ returns. Also, it is important to learn who the Enemy is. Christ identified them in the 19th Chapter. And Christ also pointed out about the Fig Tree which is the third part to gaining the key of David and the Seal of God.

Rev 5:8-9 And when he had taken the book, the four beasts and four and twenty elders fell down before the Lamb, having every one of them harps, and golden vials full of odours, which are The prayers of saints. 9 And they sung a new song, saying, Thou art worthy to take the book, and to open the seals thereof: for thou wast slain, and hast redeemed us to God by thy blood out of every kindred, and tongue, and people, and nation;

FIRST SEAL   John in Revelations:

Rev 6:2 And I saw, and behold a white horse: and he that sat on him had a bow; and a crown was given unto him: and he went forth conquering, and to conquer.

BOW: NT:5115 toxon (tox'-on); from the base of NT:5088; a bow (apparently as the simplest fabric):

CROWN: NT:4735 stephanos (stef'-an-os); from an apparently primary stepho (to twine or wreathe); a chaplet (as a badge of royalty, a prize in the public games or a symbol of honor generally; but more conspicuous and elaborate than the simple fillet, NT:1238), literally or figuratively:

CONQUER AND CONQUERING: is the same word in Greek. NT:3528 nikao (nik-ah'-o); from NT:3529; to subdue (literally or figuratively): - **conquer, overcome, prevail, get the victory.**

We have a cheap imitation, like a man standing in purple and scarlet priests robe, preaching and teaching great things that really feel good, standing in a huge awesome building with stained glass. Surely this great man "of god" wouldn't deceive us? Would he?

The LAMB who is worthy will tell us.

FIRST SEAL OPENED: Jesus speaking. Mark 13:5-6 And Jesus answering them began to say, **Take heed lest any man deceive** you: 6 For many shall come in my name, saying, I am Christ; (Christian) and shall deceive many.

SECOND SEAL: John in Revelations. Rev 6:4 And there went out another horse that was red: and power was given to him that sat thereon to **take peace from the earth, and that they should kill one another: and there was given unto him a great sword.**

Mark 13:7 Jesus Speaking.

7 And when ye shall hear of wars and rumors of wars, be ye not troubled: for such things must needs be; but the end shall not be yet.

Wars and rumors of wars, WWI and WWII and then rumors of nuclear annihilation. The COLD War.

THIRD SEAL: John in Revelations.

> Rev 6:6 And I heard a voice in
> the midst of the four beasts say,
> **A measure of wheat for a penny,**
> **and three measures of barley for**
> **a penny; and see thou hurt not**
> **the oil and the wine.**

A penny was a days earnings then. A loaf
of bread for a days wages. How much do
you really have left after you pay your
mortgage, car payment, credit cards and
taxes? That is your days wage.

THIRD SEAL: Jesus speaking.

> Mark 13:8 For nation shall rise
> against nation, and kingdom
> against kingdom: and there shall
> be earthquakes in divers places,
> and there shall be famines and
> troubles: **these are the**
> **beginnings of sorrows.** As in
> birth pains.

RISE: NT:1453   egeiro (eg-i'-ro);
probably akin to the base of NT:58
(through the idea of collecting one's
faculties); to waken   NT:58   agora (ag-
or-ah'); from ageiro (to gather;
probably akin to NT:1453); properly, the
town-square (as a place of public
resort); by implication, **a market or**
thoroughfare: - market (-place), street.

AGAINST: NT:1909 epi (ep-ee'); a primary
preposition; properly, meaning

superimposition (of time, place, order, etc.) NT:1909 - about (the times), above, after, **against, among, as long as (touching), at, beside**, have charge of, (be-, [wherefore-]), in (a place, as much as, the time of, -to), (because) of, (up-) on (behalf of), over, (by, for) the space of, through (-out), (un-) to (-ward), with. In compounds it retains essentially the same import, at, upon, etc. (literally or figuratively).

Nation standing alongside nation in the market place. This is NAFTA and the NWO with free world trade. Nation is referring to what we call the third world nations and Kingdoms are the Free world Christian Kingdoms.

FOURTH SEAL: John in Revelations.

Rev 6:8 And I looked, and behold a pale horse: and his name that sat on him was Death, and Hell followed with him. And **power was given unto them over the fourth part of the earth, to kill with sword, and with hunger, and with death, and with the beasts of the earth.**

The four parts of the Earth and the **Beasts** of the Earth are the same as the four horsemen and the four hidden dynasties, of; Religion, Economics, Politics and Education, whereby Satan's children have deceived and misguided God's children into believing their false teachings. This same thing happened to Eve in the Garden.

Famine and Hunger causes physical and spiritual starvation and then death both spiritually and physically.

> Amos 8:11-12 Behold, the days come, **saith the Lord GOD, that I will send a famine in the land, not a famine of bread, nor a thirst for water, but of hearing the words of the LORD:** 12 And they shall wander from sea to sea, and from the north even to the east, **they shall run to and fro to seek the word of the LORD, and shall not find it.**

Their power to kill with the sword means using the Word of God to deceive and spin into a false truth that kills the soul, and if this isn't enough they starve the children by teaching lies and traditions that make void the true saving grace of our LORD. **This causes death** to the spiritual man within as God's children are led to worship false gods, gods that came newly up by men and have no life in them and the Beasts of the Earth like the Banking and Economic System bringing God's children into Debt and Bondage to them.

FIFTH SEAL: John in Revelations.

> Rev 6:9-10 And when He had opened the fifth seal, I saw under the altar the souls of them that were slain for the word of God, and for the testimony which they held: 10 And they cried with a loud voice, saying, **How long, O Lord, holy and true, dost thou**

not judge and avenge our blood on
them that dwell on the earth?

Jesus speaking:

Mark 13:9-13 But take heed to
yourselves: for they shall
deliver you up to councils; and
in the synagogues ye shall be
beaten: and ye shall be brought
before rulers and kings for my
sake, for a testimony against
them.10 And the gospel must first
be published among all nations.

God will see to it that all will hear
the Gospel in their own TONGUE as the
Holy Spirit speaks through those who are
delivered up.

11 But when they shall lead you,
and deliver you up, take no
thought beforehand what ye shall
speak, neither do ye premeditate:
but whatsoever shall be given you
in that hour, that speak ye: for
it is not ye that speak, but the
Holy Ghost. =(Spirit)

**Now we come to the 6th seal. This is
Satan's appearing with all signs and
wonders.**

Rev 6:12-17; 12 And I beheld when
he had opened the **sixth seal**,
and, lo, there was a great
earthquake; and the sun became
black as sackcloth of hair, and
the moon became as blood; 13 And
the **stars of heaven fell unto the
earth**, even as a fig tree casteth

her untimely figs, when she is shaken of a mighty wind.
14 And the heaven departed as a scroll when it is rolled together; and every mountain and island were moved out of their places. 15 And the kings of the earth, and the great men, and the rich men, and the chief captains, and the mighty men, and every bondman, and every free man, hid themselves in the dens and in the rocks of the mountains; 16 And said to the mountains and rocks, Fall on us, and **hide us from the face of him that sitteth on the throne, and from the wrath of the Lamb:** 17 For the great day of his wrath is come; and who shall be able to stand?

God's wrath is the sending of the Antichrist to come and chastise his children of disobedience by taking all into captivity so that in the end they might know who LORD GOD ALMIGHTY is. God will show signs and wonders as He did before Pharaoh in Egypt so that all may know that he alone is LORD and there is none other.

Jesus opening the 6th seal.

SIXTH SEAL: Jesus speaking
Matt:13 12 Now the brother shall betray the brother to death, (Death is one of Satan's names. He will be calling himself Christ and God when he appears this time) and the father the son; and children shall rise up

against their parents, and shall
cause them to be put to death.
13 And ye shall be hated of all
men for my name's sake: but he
that shall endure unto the end,
the same shall be saved.
Because they will believe Satan
is Christ. Mark 13:14-22 14 But
when ye shall see the
abomination of desolation,
spoken of by Daniel the prophet,
standing where it ought not,
(let him that readeth
understand,) then let them that
be in Judea flee to the
mountains:

Lets go to Daniel and the setting up of
the false one.

First lets see what Daniel the Prophet
said that Christ is referring to?

Dan 12:11-13 And from the time
that the daily sacrifice shall be
taken away, and the abomination
that maketh desolate set up,
there shall be a thousand two
hundred and ninety days.
12 **Blessed is he that waiteth**,
and cometh to the thousand three
hundred and five and thirty days.
13 But go thou thy way till the
end be: for thou shalt rest, and
stand in thy lot at the end of
the days.

The taking away of the daily sacrifice
is that they will be taking communion to
the False Christ instead of the TRUE
Christ. The abomination is Satan calling

himself Christ and God, sitting in the Holy Temple which really belongs to GOD ALMIGHTY.
Bad move buddy!

This does not say blessed is he that is raptured out of here. It says blessed is he who waited until the end.

Now speaking of the Anti - instead of Christ and his false angels of light disguised as ministers of righteousness (2Cor. 11:14-15).

Dan 11:31- And arms shall stand on his part, and **they shall pollute the sanctuary of strength, and shall take away the daily sacrifice**, and **they shall place the abomination that maketh desolate**. 32 And such as do wickedly against the covenant shall he corrupt by flatteries: **but the people that do know their God shall be strong,** and do exploits.

Back to Jesus speaking:

Mark 13: 15 And let him that is on the housetop not go down into the house, neither enter therein, to take any thing out of his house:16 And let him that is in the field not turn back again for to take up his garment. 17 But woe to them that are with child, and to them that give suck in those days! 18 And pray ye that your flight be not in the winter.

180

Don't even pack your bags, time is that short.

Woe to those that are impregnated with Satan's false doctrine, thinking he is the true Christ, worshiping Satan's image and are nursing along Satan's deceptions. Pray that you are not harvested out of season like raptured before the true Christ returns.

19 For **in those days shall be affliction (G-2347:thlipsis, anguish, persecution) such as was not from the beginning of the creation** which God created unto this time, neither shall be. 20 And except that the Lord had shortened those days, no flesh should be saved: but for the elect's sake, whom he hath chosen, he hath shortened the days.

21 And then if any man shall say to you, Lo, here is Christ; or, lo, he is there; believe him not: 22 For false Christ's and false prophets shall rise, and shall shew signs and wonders, to seduce, if it were possible, even the elect.

SEVENTH SEAL:

Rev 8:1-2 And when he had opened the seventh seal, there was silence in heaven about the space of half an hour. 2 And I saw the seven angels which stood before God; and

181

to them were given **seven trumpets**.

Read how Joshua took Jericho and the 7 trumpets along with the final shout on the 7th day as the priests blew all 7 trumpets. (Joshua 6: 3-6)

Jesus Speaking of the 7th and last seal, trumpet and vial.

> Mark 13:24-26 24 But in those days, **after that tribulation**, the sun shall be darkened, and the moon shall not Give her light, 25 And the stars of heaven shall fall, and the powers that are in heaven shall be shaken. 26 And **then shall they see the Son of man coming in the clouds with great power and Glory.**

> 1 Thess 4:16 **For the Lord himself shall descend from heaven with a shout, with the voice of the archangel, and with the trump of God: and the dead in Christ shall rise first KJV** Amen

Conclusion: we should know about the three Earth Ages and why we are here in this Flesh Earth Age. We should know who the tares are (Mat: 13 7) from Cain to today. What our true heritage is. Know the parable of the Fig Tree and that the False Christ comes first. If you still don't get it order free tape on Mark of Beast from Shepherd's Chapel at end of book.

Chapter XVI

What does Born Again really mean ?

This same question was asked by one of
the most prestigious church leaders.
Let's see what Jesus says to him.

> John 3:4-5 Nicodemus saith unto
> him, How can a man be born when
> he is old? can he enter the
> second time into his mother's
> womb, and be born?
> 5 Jesus answered, Verily,
> verily, I say unto thee, Except
> a man be born of water and of
> the Spirit, he cannot enter
> into the kingdom of God. 6 That
> which is born of the flesh is
> flesh; and that which is born
> of the Spirit is spirit. KJV

Born of water= from the womb breaking
fourth from water into our earthly flesh
bodies in life. This is what being
baptized is symbolic of. Going under the
water and coming up into life eternal in
Jesus Christ.

Born of spirit= returning back to the
Father who placed our spirit man in the
flesh.

> John 3:7 Marvel not that I said
> unto thee, Ye must be born
> again. KJV (Born from above).

Born: NT:1080 gennao (ghcn-nah'-o); from
a variation of NT:1085; to procreate
(properly, of the father, but by
extension of the mother); figuratively,

to regenerate: Again in Greek:NT:509 anothen (an'-o-then); from NT:507; from above; by analogy, from the first; by implication, anew: KJV - **from above**, again, from the beginning (very first), the top.

Nicodemus did not know the scriptures. He should have known about; the three earth ages The one third of God's children that followed Satan in the first earth age, the decree that all of God's children are to go through the flesh womb (water) into the flesh in this Earth and Heaven Age to decide who they are going to revere and follow. That they are to die (experience dying) and be born, regenerate back into their spirit bodies.

Here is a second witness to this.

> 1 Cor 15:44 It is sown a
> natural body; it is raised a
> spiritual body. There is a
> natural body, and there is a
> spiritual body.

> Eccl 12:7 Then shall the dust
> return to the earth as it was:
> and the spirit shall return
> unto God who gave it.

> John 12:24 Verily, verily, I
> say unto you, Except a corn of
> wheat fall into the ground and
> die, it abideth alone: but if
> it die, it bringeth forth much
> fruit.

184

John 12:25-26 He that loveth
his life shall lose it; and he
that hateth his life in this
world shall keep it unto life
eternal.

Why would one hate or love less his life
in this world? Love the LORD more!

Because he realizes that we are spirit
men, held within this flesh which is
weak, confined, stupid, sickly and not
able to be with God who is spirit. We
miss our home and Father and family. We
are strangers in a strange land.

26 If any man serve me, let him
follow me; and where I am,
there shall also my servant be:
if any man serve me, him will
my Father honour. KJV

The angels, Nephilim(sons of God) who
left Heaven and went after the daughters
of Adam without going through the water
(womb) into the flesh went directly
against God's decree.
They also were trying to stop God's plan
of salvation of his children by
interfering with the pedigree birth of
Christ by intermingling with the seed of
HaAdam (the man Adam).

Gen 6:1-2:1 And it came to pass,
when men began to multiply on
the face of the earth, and
daughters were born unto them, 2
That the sons of God saw the
daughters of men that they were

185

fair; and they took them wives
of all which they chose.

And what was the result of the sons of
God, fallen angels breeding with the
sons of men?

Gen 6:4 There were giants in the
earth in those days; and also
after that, when the sons of God
came in unto the daughters of
men, and they bare children to
them, the same became mighty men
which were of old, men of
renown.

WERE OF OLD: OT:5769 `owlam (o-lawm');
or `olam (o-lawm'); from OT:5956;
properly, concealed, i.e. the vanishing
point; generally, time out of mind (past
or future), i.e. (practically) eternity;
frequentatively, adverbial (especially
with prepositional prefix) always:

2 Peter 2:4-5 For if God spared
not the angels that sinned, but
cast them down to hell, and
delivered them into chains of
darkness, to be reserved unto
judgment;

2 Peter 2:5 And spared not the
old world, but saved Noah the
eighth person, a preacher of
righteousness, bringing in the
flood upon the world of the
ungodly;

Why was the flood of Noah? 1.) Because
these Sons of God went against Fathers
decree, that all will go through the

flesh. 2.) To rid the earth of the EVIL FALLEN ONES and their offspring. And 3.) to bring forth the unmingled seed line of Noah, through whom the unblemished Christ would come to save God's children from Satan and his angels. There is a controversy and it has been going on since before Adam, all the way back into the first Earth Age when $1/3^{rd}$ of God's children followed Satan, his false doctrine and his kings rather than our true Father (Rev.12 4). Nothing new under the sun. This Earth Age is so that all shall have an equal and fair chance to make their minds up as to who they really want to follow, born without knowledge of the Age that was.

Jude 6 And the <u>angels which kept not their first estate, but left their own habitation</u>, he hath reserved in everlasting chains under darkness unto the judgment of the great day.

See, Christ, God, wouldn't ask His children to do something He wouldn't do himself. Christ came through the womb (water), was baptized by John in the water, died and resurrected into Spirit Man God where He lives forever and awaits His children's return to Him.

A parallel exists between Heaven and Earth. We are commanded to go through the womb (water) into flesh life, die in the flesh and return in our spirit men back to God.

We are commanded to be Baptized into water where our rising from the water signifies our resurrection with Christ into the Spirit man, washed in His blood, cleansed and Holy before our Father.

All are to be born from above.

We are to experience death of the flesh as we have never died in our spirit men.

> Heb 9:27 And as it is appointed unto men once to die, but after this the judgment:

This experience in the flesh shall show us what it would be like in our spirit men if we were to die (perish) at the Great White Throne judgment at the end of the Millenium, should we still refuse to listen to, revere and follow the LORD even after 1000 years of teachings without the influences of Satan and his cronies.

If you do not learn during the 1000 years?

> Rev 20:7-8 And when the thousand years are expired, Satan shall be loosed out of his prison, 8 And shall go out to deceive the nations which are in the four quarters of the earth, Gog and Magog, to gather them together to battle: the number of whom is as the sand of the sea KJV.

Then comes the end.

Chapter XVII

Where the Dead are
and
what does the flesh have to do
with all this?

We have a Spirit body and an earthly body as the Holy Spirit says it best through Paul.

We are going to learn that when our terrestrial body dies our spirit or celestial body returns to the Father who placed it in our flesh bodies.

1 Cor 15:40
40 There are also celestial bodies, and bodies terrestrial: but the glory of the celestial is one, and the glory of the terrestrial is another.

Celestial. NT:2032 epouranios (ep-oo-ran'-ee-os); from NT:1909 and NT:3772; **above** the sky: KJV - celestial, (in) heaven (-ly), high.

Our Celestial man is born again which means born from above when we are conceived and placed into the flesh or terrestrial body which is earthly vessel.

Terrestrial. NT:1919 epigeios (ep-ig'-i-os); from NT:1909 and NT:1093; worldly (physically or morally): KJV - **earthly,** in earth, terrestrial.

1 Cor 15:42-45 So also is the resurrection of the dead. It is sown in corruption; it is raised in incorruption:43 It is sown in dishonor; it is raised in glory: it is sown in weakness; (of the flesh) it is raised in power:44 <u>It is sown a natural body; it is raised a spiritual body. There is a natural body, and there is a spiritual body.</u>
45 And so it is written, The first man Adam was made a living soul; the last Adam was made a quickening spirit.

Looking at the witnesses about the spirit man within and what happens when we die.

God said:Heb.9 27 **And as <u>it is appointed unto men once to die,</u> (in the flesh) but after this the judgment:**

And Again:
2 Cor 5:6-8 Therefore we are always confident, knowing that, **<u>whilst we are at home in the body, we are absent from the Lord:</u>**7(For we walk by faith, not by sight:)8 **<u>We are confident, I say, and willing rather to be absent from the body, and to be present with the Lord</u>**.

Here is what God said to Adam in the Garden regarding Adam's earthly body.

Gen 3:19 In the sweat of thy
face shalt thou eat bread, till
thou return unto the ground; for
out of it wast thou taken: **for
dust thou art, and unto dust
shalt thou return.**

Eccl 3:20 All go unto one place;
**all are of the dust, and all
turn to dust again.**

Eccl 12:6-7 Or ever the silver
cord be loosed, or the golden
bowl be broken, or the pitcher
be broken at the fountain, or
the wheel broken at the cistern.
**7 Then shall the dust return to
the earth as it was: and the
spirit shall return unto God who
gave it.**

Luke 20:34-38 And Jesus
answering said unto them, The
children of this world marry,
and are given in marriage:

35 But they which shall be
accounted worthy to obtain that
world, and the resurrection from
the dead, neither marry, nor are
given in marriage:

Why? No need to replenish the Earth with
flesh because we are finished with the
Flesh.
36 **Neither can they die any
more: for they are equal unto
the angels; and are the
children of God**, being the
children of the resurrection.

191

How does one become accounted worthy to obtain that world?

> 37 Now that the dead are raised, even Moses shewed at the bush, when he calleth the Lord the God of Abraham, and the God of Isaac, and the God of Jacob. 38 **For he is not a God of the dead, but of the living: for all live unto him.**

And Jesus said:

> John 11:26
> 26 And **whosoever liveth and believeth in me shall never die**. Believest thou this?

And again Jesus said:

> John 3:14-15
> 14 And **as Moses lifted up the serpent in the wilderness,** even **so must the Son of man be lifted up**: 15 That whosoever **believeth in him should not perish, but have eternal life**.

What was the serpent in the wilderness on the pole all about?

SERPENT: NT:3789 ophis (of'-is); probably from NT:3700 (through the idea of sharpness of vision); a snake, figuratively **(as a type of sly cunning) an artful malicious person,)** especially Satan:
Serpent: OT:5172 nachash (naw-khash'); a primitive root; properly, to hiss,

192

i.e. **whisper a (magic) spell**;
generally, to prognosticate:

Could it be that the people realized
that they were following traditions of
men rather than the TRUE WORD OF GOD?

> Num 21:7-8 Therefore the people
> came to Moses, and said, We
> have sinned, for we have spoken
> against the LORD, and against
> thee; pray unto the LORD, that
> he take away the serpents
> **(cunning artful malicious
> persons who is whispering magic
> spells)** from us. And Moses
> prayed for the people.
> 8 And the LORD said unto Moses,
> **Make thee a fiery serpent, and
> set it upon a pole:** and it
> shall come to pass, that **every
> one that is bitten, when he
> looketh (Heb. Ra ah, take heed,
> see, consider) upon it, shall
> live.** (Gr. chay a, to revive).

Jesus Christ was also lifted up on a pole
cross. Are we considering our ways?

> 27 And as it is appointed unto
> men once to die, (in the flesh)
> but after this the judgment:

Why only once? I thought I lived before?

Since evil spirits as well as our own
spirits have never died, evil spirits
can tell you about places and things
that happened way back in History with
great detail. Think about it? Did you
know that, although our memories were

wiped clean when we came into the flesh we actually witnessed Christ's crucifixion as well as the Flood and all of History?

It is written that we were with God. **and the spirit shall return unto God who gave it.**

When you learn and know the rest of the story you will understand that as Spirit beings we never experienced death. God did destroy the first Earth and Heaven age, took all of His children home with Him (evidenced by Dinosaur bones and lost Atlantis etc.)We were all spirit beings, Angels, stones of fire or Stars as we are called. God then decreed that we were to all go through the flesh, without any knowledge of the Age that WAS and make our minds up who we are going to follow; God and His holy righteousness or Satan and his unrighteous unholiness. Then we are to experience what it feels like to die – but only the flesh dies. This is like a warning that this is what will happen to your Soul and Spirit Man at the end of the Millenium if you still refuse God.

Well then, what does God require from us in our weak and restricted flesh bodies?

> Mic 6:8 He hath shewed thee, O man, what is good; and **what doth the LORD require of thee, but to do justly, and to love mercy, and to walk humbly with thy God**?

To do justly and love mercy and walk
humbly with God one must have to know
God. How do we do that?   How do we know
His ways and who He is?

Hos 6 6: for I desired mercy
(Heb. Che ced, your love), and
not sacrifice; and the
knowledge of God more than
burnt offerings.

John 1:1 In the beginning was
the Word, and the Word was with
God, **and the Word was God.**

John 1:14 **And the Word was made
flesh, and dwelt among us**, (and
we beheld his glory, the glory
as of the only begotten of the
Father,) full of grace and
truth.

Note: the Serpent on a stick is our
MEDICAL SYMBOL OF TODAY. Have we
forgotten Christ crucified and are we
looking at the old serpent on a pole?

2Kings: 18 1-7 Hezekiah, the last
great King of Judah broke down the
Brazen Serpent, trusted in the LORD
and followed the LORD'S commandments.

Who put the serpent back up?
How subtle is this?

Chapter XVIII

Was Jesus Christ a radical and Politically incorrect ? Who murdered Him and what was their agenda?

We will learn that Jesus came to us as a man in the flesh, just the same as we are.
That Jesus was of the perfect King lineage and Levitical Priests lineage all the way from Adam.
That Satan, his angels and his children tried to stop Christ from coming. This is the reason for most of the wars in the Bible. Satan was trying to divide, weaken, subvert and pervert God's plan of redemption and salvation and Satan is still working on his own agenda this very day. This is the reason Herod murdered all children two years old and under that were in Bethlehem. Who do you think Herod's father and master was (Matt. 2:16)?
That Jesus told the self appointed priests right to their faces that although they claim to be children of Abraham, they are Satan's children. (John. 8: 42-44).
That Jesus taught the perfect laws of liberty and freedom which was in direct opposition to the teachings of the churches who wanted to hold God's children in bondage to themselves, with do this and don't do that and traditions that make the words of God void, of none effect and weaken God's children. Why do

you think that today our teachers and churches do not teach the word of God as it is written? It is politically not correct and goes against all traditions that we have been taught.

Oh Oh! Have they been deceiving us all along? They are in big trouble if the WORD gets out.

Here is the prophesy about Christ coming from the TORAH. There are many many prophesies of Christ's coming within the Torah. Why and how did those who claim to be Jews miss this and still look for another?

> Deut 18:15 The LORD thy God will raise up unto thee a Prophet from the midst of thee, of thy brethren, like unto me; unto him ye shall hearken; KJV

We are starting to get to the root reason why the Church wanted to and did murder Christ?

He took away their thunder; Christ was teaching the perfect laws of liberty, not bondage to a church, a tradition, or to any man. People began to follow Christ and the Church began loosing "tithes" $$$$$ WHICH IS ALSO TRANSLATED INTO LARGE CONGREGATIONS AND POWER OVER THE PEOPLE FOR THEIR OWN WILL, NOT GOD'S WILL.

Here is what Jesus said.

Luke 4:18-19 **The Spirit of the Lord is upon me, because he hath anointed me to** preach the gospel to the poor; **he hath sent me to** heal the brokenhearted, **to preach** deliverance to the captives, **and recovering of** sight to the blind, **to** set at liberty **them that are bruised,19 To preach the acceptable year of the Lord.**
Luke 4:20-21 And he closed the book, and he gave it again to the minister, and sat down. And the eyes of all them that were in the synagogue were fastened on him. 21 And he began to say unto them, **This day is this scripture fulfilled in your ears.**

If you have read about the three Earth ages, then you will realize why we are here in this flesh Earth Age by decree from God.
Jesus / Emanuel (God with us), as our true King and Lord of Lords would not ask us to go through this flesh without going through it Himself.

What makes a real leader?

How would He be able to understand the temptations, trials and tribulations we go through if He had not done the same and been tempted by all the same things we are, yet He alone remained unblemished and righteous?

How else would He be able to counsel us
as to how to deal with all of this?
How could he be our high Priest of
the order of Melchizedek?
How could anyone else have become the
perfect unblemished sacrifice for our
sins, first born, first raised from the
dead and our kinsman redeemer?

**Here we document that Jesus Christ is
of the perfect lineage as King and
Priest all the way back to Adam.**

Luke 1:5 There was in the days
of Herod, the king of Judaea, a
certain priest named Zacharias,
of the course of Abia: and his
wife was of the daughters of
Aaron, and her name was
Elisabeth. She is John the
Baptists Mother.

Luke 1:13 But the angel said
unto him, Fear not, Zacharias:
for thy prayer is heard; and **thy
wife Elisabeth shall bear thee a
son, and thou shalt call his
name John.**
Luke 1:30-33 And the angel said
unto her, Fear not, Mary: for
thou hast found favour with God.
31 And, behold, thou shalt
conceive in thy womb, and bring
forth a son, and shalt call his
name JESUS.
32 He shall be great, and shall
be called the Son of the
Highest: and the Lord God shall
give unto him the throne of his
father David:
33 And he shall reign over the

house of Jacob for ever; and of his kingdom there shall be no end.

Luke 1:36 And, behold, **thy cousin Elisabeth, she hath also conceived a son in her old age**: and this is the sixth month with her, who was called barren. KJV

Here we see; that Elizabeth's husband "Zacharias" was a Levitical Priest. By statute also Elizabeth had to be a Levite in order to be married to a Priest. We also see that Mary was Elizabeth's Cousin which means that Mary is also of the Priest/Levite Lineage. Now we will go through the Lineage which is a little tedious until after we finish it so stay with us.

Matt 1:17 So all the generations from Abraham to David are fourteen generations; and from David until the carrying away into Babylon are fourteen generations; and from the carrying away into Babylon unto Christ are fourteen generations.

Luke 3:23-4:1 And Jesus himself began to be about thirty years of age, being (as was supposed) (this means in laws) the son of Joseph, which was the son of Heli,

We will skip ahead a little.

31 Which was the son of Melea, which was the son of Menan, which was the son of Mattatha, which

was **the son of Nathan, which was
the son of David,**
32 **Which was the son of Jesse,**
which was the son of Obed, which
was the son of Booz, which was
the son of Salmon, which was the
son of Naasson,

We are going to skip ahead or should I
say back to Adam to document the
genealogy of Christ.

36 Which was the son of Cainan,
which was the son of Arphaxad,
which was the son of Sem, which
was the son of Noe, which was the
son of Lamech,
37 Which was the son of
Mathusala, which was the son of
Enoch, which was the son of
Jared, which was the son of
Maleleel, which was the son of
Cainan, 38 Which was the son of
Enos, which was the son of Seth,
**which was the son of Adam, which
was the son of God.**

**This is the lineage of Christ all the
way back to Adam.**

Do not miss the fact that Jesus was not
of the lineage of Joseph. Jesus was the
Son of God by the Holy Spirit;
therefore, this lineage is Joseph's In-
laws or Mary's family which is the King
Line and the Levitical Priest Line. You
may understand the Levitical priest line
by the fact that Elizabeth, Mary's
cousin was a Levite woman and married to
a Levite Priest, Zechariah.

JESUS IS NOW GOING RADICAL BECAUSE HE IS TEACHING THE TRUTH!

Let's watch as Jesus goes radical and politically not correct.

In the Garden of Eden we are shown that Eve had fraternal twins, Cain and Abel. Cain from the Tree of Good and Evil, SATAN and Abel from ADAM.

If you do not believe this is true, listen to what Christ says to the Pharisees and Sadducees, the church leaders and read chapter of Apple in the Garden.

> John 8:42-44 Jesus said unto them, **(the Pharisees)** If God were your Father, ye would love me: for I proceeded forth and came from God; neither came I of myself, but he sent me.43 Why do ye not understand my speech? even because ye cannot hear my word.44 **Ye are of your father the devil, and the lusts of your father ye will do. He was a murderer from the beginning, and abode not in the truth, because there is no truth in him. When he speaketh a lie, he speaketh of his own: for he is a liar, and the father of it.** KJV

Who was the first murderer? CAIN!

And in another place Jesus taught about the Tares and the Wheat:

Matt 13:38-39 **The field is the world; the good seed are the children of the kingdom; but the tares are the children of the wicked one; 39 The enemy that sowed them is the devil;** the harvest is the end of the world; and the reapers are the angels.

Did you know that if you put a goat in with a flock of sheep, the sheep will always follow the goat if they have no Shepherd with them. Just a thought from a sheep farmer.

Do you follow the Shepherd or a Goat?

Matt 25:32 And before him shall be gathered all nations: and he shall separate them one from another, as a shepherd divideth his sheep from the goats: KJV

If you think Star Wars was good, the more you learns of the truth about who we really are, where we came from, who our real Father is, this is way better than Star Wars which is soon coming to it's fullness. Better get your sword ready.

You "see" there is good and evil. We are violators of the perfect laws of God's Universe. Call it the law of Karma if you like. God wrote His laws through Moses. Mostly simple rules of righteousness like; If you borrow something from your neighbor and you break it, replace it. If we had followed God's rules there would be no poverty, no illness, no murderers, no rapists, no sorcerers and no bondage to an unholy unrighteous debt and taxation system among us. Well along we come, unwilling in the flesh to keep those laws. What then?

> Matt 6:33 But seek ye first the kingdom of God, and his righteousness; and all these things shall be added unto you.

There were many scared sheep and bullocks that were sacrificed to take away the curses of violating God's perfect laws. We couldn't even do that right. Priests became lazy, scribes took over the temple and things became messed up. As a result God's children were taken captive by the King of Babylon (a type of Anti-Christ), then scattered throughout the Earth. We were in bad shape. God then sent His Son, Jesus Christ to become the sacrifice and intermediator for one and all times as High Priest to remove the curses upon His children for violating the perfect laws of the Universe as God had set it up, in righteousness and holiness to Him. First His original 12 tribes called Israel, then all of the world, whosoever would understand this and believe.

This is what Christ said first:

> Matt 10:5-6 These twelve Jesus sent forth, and commanded them, saying, Go not into the way of the Gentiles, and into any city of the Samaritans enter ye not: 6

But **go rather to the lost sheep
of the house of Israel**. KJV

The first called were all twelve tribes.
Guess what? They didn't all believe and
the wedding feast was lacking guests.

Matt 22:3 And sent forth his
servants to call them that were
bidden to the wedding: and they
would not come.

Then after Christ was crucified for the
sins of the World. The door was opened
to anyone who would hear and come.

Matt 22:9-10 Go ye therefore
into the highways, and as many
as ye shall find, bid to the
marriage.10 So those servants
went out into the highways, and
gathered together all as many as
they found, both bad and good:
and the wedding was furnished
with guests.

John 3:16-17 For God so loved
the world, that he gave his only
begotten Son, that whosoever
believeth in him should not
perish, but have everlasting
life. 17 For God sent not his
Son into the world to condemn
the world; but that the world
through him might be saved. KJV

Statements to ponder:

What will the preachers say when one
shows up calling himself Christ and god
and no one is raptured out of here?

This false one will be showing miracles and wonders (Rev: 13 13). He will claim that the enemy and the tribulation is coming soon and everyone must get ready to fight against this enemy. By the way, the enemy this false one will be speaking of is the true LORD and KING of KINGS and LORD of Hosts.

The preachers will turn over everyone to follow the imposter. They will fall on their knees to him. See, even Jesus taught about this apostasy or falling away and what the preachers would do. Here it is.

> John 10:12-13 But he that is an hireling, and not the shepherd, whose own the sheep are not, seeth the wolf coming, and leaveth the sheep, and fleeth: and the wolf catcheth them, and scattereth the sheep. 13 The hireling fleeth, because he is an hireling, and careth not for the sheep. KJV

The word hireling in the Greek: NT:3408 misthos (mis-thos'); apparently a **primary word; pay for services** (literally or figuratively), good or bad: KJV - hire, reward, wages.

In it for the Money. I always look to what it is that the person speaks most about and that tells me what is foremost in his mind as in what fruit tree I am looking at. Is it a warm fuzzy as in flesh or is it from the Holy Spirit, the true word of God?

More food for thought: Did you ever hear a minister or priest teach the prophets like Hosea?

Hos 5:1 **Hear ye this, O priests**; and hearken, ye house of Israel; and give ye ear, O house of the king; for judgment is toward you, because ye have been a snare on Mizpah, = (watch **tower=Samaria**) and a net spread upon Tabor = (**broken hearted, torn and wounded**).

Why? By teaching traditions of man and not the TRUTH by God's word chapter by chapter and verse by verse, rightly dividing the word and bringing fourth that which was written in truth and righteousness.

Here is a little more of what the Spirit says through the Prophets.

Mic.3:9-12: 9 Hear this, I pray you, ye heads of the house of Jacob = (**all 12 tribes**), and princes of the house of Israel, that abhor judgment, and pervert all equity. 10 They build up Zion = (**the mountain of God**) with blood, and Jerusalem = (**city of peace**) with iniquity. 11 The heads thereof judge for reward = (**payoffs $$$**), and the priests

You leave our people defenseless and unable to stand against the fiery darts of the evil one.

<u>Shame on you who call yourselves</u>
<u>priests and judges and leaders.</u>

<u>thereof teach for hire</u> =
(Money$$$), and the <u>prophets</u>
<u>thereof divine for money</u>: yet
will they lean upon the LORD,
and say, Is not the LORD among
us? <u>none evil can come upon us.</u>
(this is a lie, like we're
going to be raptured out of
here and will not see the
tribulation).12 herefore shall
Zion for your sake be plowed as
a field, and Jerusalem shall
become heaps, and the mountain
of the house as the <u>high places</u>
<u>of the forest</u> **(where false gods**
were worshiped).

This is where the baal worship took
place to false gods, like
Ashtar/Ashtoreth "Easter" along with
orgies of fertility and unholy
sacrifices).

Here is some wisdom about this tradition
and how it came into our churches along
with the symbol of fertility, the Easter
bunny.

ASHTORETH:
(ash'-to-reth), (ash-to reth)
(`ashtoreth; plural `ashtaroth;
Astarte):
1. Name and Origin
2. Attributes of the Goddess
3. Ashtoreth as a Moon-goddess
4. The Local Ashtaroth The name of the
supreme goddess of Canaan and the female

counterpart of **Baal.**

1. Name and Origin: The name and cult of the goddess were derived from Babylonia, where Istar represented the evening and morning stars and was accordingly androgynous in origin. Under Semitic influence, however, she became solely female, but retained a memory of her primitive character by standing, alone among the Assyro-Bab goddesses, on a footing of equality with the male divinities. From Babylonia the worship of the goddess was carried to the Semites of the West, and in most instances the feminine suffix was attached to her name; where this was not the case the deity was regarded as a male. On the Moabite Stone, for example, 'Ashtar is identified with Chemosh, and in the inscriptions of southern Arabia 'Athtar is a god. On the other hand, in Atar-gatis or Derketo (2 Macc 12:26), Atar, without the feminine suffix, is identified with the goddess 'Athah or 'Athi (Greek Gatis). The cult of the Greek Aphrodite in Cyprus was borrowed from that of Ashtoreth; whether the Greek name also is a modification of Ashtoreth, as has often been maintained, is doubtful.

2. Attributes of the Goddess: In Babylonia and **Assyria Istar was the goddess of love and war.** An old Babylonian legend related how the descent of Istar into Hades in search of her dead husband, Tammuz, was followed by the cessation of marriage and birth in both earth and heaven, while the temples of the goddess at Nineveh and Arbela, around which the two cities

afterward grew up, were dedicated to her
as the goddess of war. As such she
appeared to one of Assur-bani-pal's
seers and encouraged the Assyrian king
to march against Elam. The other
goddesses of Babylonia, who were little
more than reflections of the god, tended
to merge into Istar who thus became a
type of the female divinity, a
personification of the productive
principle in nature, and more especially
the mother and creatress of mankind.
The chief seat of the worship of Istar
in Babylonia was Erech, where
prostitution was practiced in her name,
and she was served with immoral rites
by bands of men and women. In Assyria,
where the warlike side of the goddess
was predominant, no such rites seem to
have been practiced, and, instead,
prophetesses were attached to her
temples to whom she delivered oracles.
3. Ashtoreth as a Moon-Goddess: In
Canaan, Ashtoreth, as distinguished from
the male 'Ashtar, dropped her warlike
attributes, but in contradistinction to
Asherah, whose name and cult had also
been imported from Assyria, became, on
the one hand, the colorless consort of
Baal, and on the other hand, a moon-
goddess. In Babylonia the moon was a
god, but after the rise of the solar
theology, when the larger number of the
Babylonian gods were resolved into forms
of the sun-god, their wives also became
solar, Ishtar, "the daughter of Sin" the
moon-god, remaining identified with the
evening-star. In Canaan, however, when
the solar theology had absorbed the
older beliefs, Baal, passing into a sun-
god and the goddess who stood at his

side becoming a representative of the moon-the pale reflection, as it were, of the sun-Ashtoreth came to be regarded as the consort of Baal and took the place of the solar goddesses of Babylonia. 4. The Local Ashtaroth: Hence there were as "many Ashtoreths" or Ashtaroth as Baals. They represented the various forms under which the goddess was worshipped in different localities (Judg 10:6; 1 Sam 7:4; 12:10, etc.). Sometimes she was addressed as Naamah, "the delightful one," Greek Astro-noe, the mother of Eshmun and the Cabeiri. The Philistines seem to have adopted her under her warlike form (1 Sam 31:10 the King James Version reading "Ashtoreth," as LXX), but she was more usually the moon-goddess (Lucian, De Dca Syr., 4; Herodian, v.6, 10), and was accordingly symbolized by the horns of a cow. (from International Standard Bible Encyclopaedia, Electronic Database Copyright (c)1996 by Biblesoft)

It therefore becomes easy for us to see how we have adopted traditions from Babylon since the original tribes were taken captive by the king of Babylon (who was a type of Antichrist, who is coming again to take us captive) and our great great ancestors lived therein.

This is written as an example to forewarn us and show us what is coming in these end times.

The LORD is going to bring your unholy and unrighteous systems down.

More about the modern day prophets (preachers) teachers and priests and Government.

Zeph 3:4 Her prophets are light and treacherous persons: **her priests have polluted the sanctuary, they have done violence to the law**.

Zech 7:4-7 Then came the word of the LORD of hosts unto me, saying, 5 **Speak unto all the people of the land, and to the priests**, saying, When ye fasted and mourned in the fifth and seventh month, even those seventy years, did ye at all fast unto me, even to me?
6 And when ye did eat, and when ye did drink, did not ye eat for yourselves, and drink for yourselves? 7 **Should ye not hear the words which the LORD hath cried by the former prophets**, When Jerusalem was inhabited and in prosperity, and the cities thereof round about her, when men inhabited the south and the plain?

Zech 7:8-13 And the word of the LORD came unto Zechariah, saying, 9 **Thus speaketh the LORD of hosts, saying, Execute true judgment, and shew mercy and compassions every man to his brother: 10 And oppress not the widow, nor the fatherless, the stranger, nor the poor; and let none of you imagine evil against**

his brother in your heart. 11 But they refused to hearken, and pulled away the shoulder, and stopped their ears, that they should not hear. 12 Yea, they made their hearts as an adamant stone, lest they should hear the law, and the words which the LORD of hosts hath sent in his spirit by the former prophets: therefore came a great wrath from the LORD of hosts. 13 Therefore <u>it is come to pass, that as he cried, and they would not hear; so they cried, and I would not hear, saith the LORD of hosts</u>: KJV

If this makes you want to know more look at this and then go to the sources within for more good food of truth.

Jer 29:8-9 For thus saith the LORD of hosts, the God of Israel; **Let not your prophets and your diviners, that be in the midst of you, deceive you, neither hearken to your dreams which ye cause to be dreamed.**

9 For they prophesy falsely unto you in my name: I have not sent them, saith the LORD.

This goes with the warnings Jesus gave also.

Mark 13:5-6 And Jesus answering them began to say, Take heed lest any man deceive you:

6 For many shall come in my name,

saying, I am Christ (Christian);
and shall deceive many. KJV

**This means check every teacher, preacher
and Christian out against the true word
of God.**

It is important to rightly divide the
word as to figures of speech, metaphors,
symbols, and proper translations from
the manuscripts.

It is wise for the serious gold miner to
purchase proper tools like a Strong's
Exhaustive Concordance and a Smith's
Bible Dictionary at least.

It should also be noted that the church
did not want the manuscripts translated
into English and performed this against
their will at the demand of the King.

There was a warning in the front of the
original King James Bibles telling you
to check out their translations if
something does not make sense. This
letter has been conveniently removed by
the publishers of late. We have added
some clips from it in this book under
the chapter on Deception.

You may send for this complete letter
from Kings Chapel or Shepherd's Chapel.

Here is another example of US missing
the mark.

CAPITAL PUNNISHMENT: The bleeding heart
Christians, as they are called, who are
against Capital Punishment are partly
right and partly wrong. They sympathize

for the convicted in that the system has become so unjust that there are many innocent people convicted by false witnesses and unjust prosecutors, law enforcement officers and lawyers. The truth of the matter is that Capital Punishment is required; however, there are rules to this. The major rule is that if we find a man who was falsely convicted by a prosecutor who hides the truth and false witnesses who aid in the innocent man's conviction we are to do to them what they had imagined to do the convicted man. Then this crap will cease to happen among us.

In a nut shell. If you lie, hide information that could prove innocence, manufacture false evidence and otherwise convict an innocent man you also will go to prison, death row, as you have determined to do to that man.

Here is the LAW from which our law came.

> Deut 19:11-13 But if any man hate his neighbour, and lie in wait (**as in premeditate**) for him, and rise up against him, and smite him mortally that he die, and fleeth into one of these cities:12 Then the elders of his city shall send and fetch him thence, and deliver him into the hand of the avenger of blood, that he may die.13 Thine eye shall not pity him, but **thou shalt put away the guilt of innocent blood from Israel, that it may go well with thee.**

215

Deut 19:15-17 One witness shall not rise up against a man for any iniquity, or for any sin, in any sin that he sinneth: **at the mouth of two witnesses, or at the mouth of three** witnesses, shall the matter be established.

16 **If a false witness rise up against any man to testify against him** that which is wrong;

17 Then both the men, between whom the controversy is, shall stand before the LORD, before the priests and the judges, which shall be in those days; Deut 19:19-20 **Then shall ye do unto him, as he had thought to have done unto his brother**: so shalt thou put the evil away from among you.20 And those which remain shall hear, and fear, and shall henceforth commit no more any such evil among you. KJV

Those who think they have gotten away with something, the just and the unjust, shall stand before the judgment seat of Christ and give account themselves.

Chapter XVIV

What does Tithing really mean?

and

What does seed have to do with tithing?

The word tithes means a tenth and is used 24 times in the Bible. . Law of tithing: Deut: 26: 12. Read; Jer. 7: 22 and Amos: 4: 4 if you really want to know how God feels about all your sacrifices. God wants us to love Him and gain knowledge of Him more than all the tithes and sacrifices, Hosea: 6 6.

So, if you are learning about God and gaining in understanding by being taught the whole TRUTH of God's words then there is where you should tithe. Would you want the mark in your right hand because you were supporting false doctrines?

If you want to go to a concert or a show, go ahead and pay for it but it is an abomination to call it a House of God.

The word tithe means a tenth or ten. It was given to the Levite Priests and out of that they took a tenth for their maintenance as they had no inheritance of land or other things of the LORD, the church fed the poor, cared for elderly like our social security, cared for the widows and maintained the Courts along with the sacrifices and offerings before God

Today our Government takes the greatest part of that tithe. We are now left to offer freely to the LORD that which we are able in thanksgiving for our wonderful blessings, being fed His word and learning truly about our Father.

This TRUTH is what sets us free from Satan's bondage and man's traditions which have held so many in bondage for so many years. Zerubbabel, Come out of her my people.

> Mal 3:8-10 Will a man rob God? Yet ye have robbed me. But ye say, **Wherein have we robbed thee? ANSWER: In tithes and offerings**. 9 Ye are cursed with a curse: for ye have robbed me, even this whole nation.10 Bring ye all the tithes into the storehouse, that there may be meat (H-2964 Terep: to supply food, as in John 21-15 **Feed my Lambs** vs. 16 **Feed my sheep**) in mine house, and prove me now herewith, saith the LORD of hosts, if I will not open you the windows of heaven, and pour you out a blessing, that there shall not be room enough to receive it. KJV

Now let us look into seed in the word of God.

The word seed is used 279 times in the Bible. It refers to fruit bearing trees, offspring, and planting the Word of God.

WARNING!! When a man tells you that seed means money, they are rip off artists and are lying to you. Whose seed do you think they are?

Gen 1:11 And God said, Let the earth bring forth grass, the herb yielding seed, and the fruit tree yielding fruit after his kind, whose **seed** is in itself, upon the earth: and it was so.

This means the seed of the tree within itself.

Gen 12:7 And the LORD appeared unto Abram, and said, Unto thy **seed** will I give this land: and there builded he an altar unto the LORD, who appeared unto him.

The LORD is not talking about Abraham's money here. He is talking about Abraham's children.

SEED in Hebrew: OT:2233 zera` (zeh'-rah); from OT:2232; seed; figuratively, fruit, plant, sowing-time, posterity: carnally, child, fruitful, seed (-time), sowing time.

Let's go to the New Testament and see what Jesus says about seed.

Luke 8:11 Now the parable is this: The seed is the word of God. Those that hear the word of the kingdom, and understandeth it

> not, then cometh the wicked one,
> and catcheth away <u>that which was</u>
> <u>sown in his heart</u>. <u>This is he</u>
> <u>which received **seed** by the way</u>
> <u>side</u>. 20 But <u>he that received the</u>
> **<u>seed</u>** <u>into stony places, the same</u>
> <u>is he that heareth the word</u>, and
> anon with joy receiveth it;---

Jesus is talking about the WORD OF GOD
not money.

Looking into more of what Jesus was
saying regarding seed as children.

> Matt 13:37-39 He answered and
> said unto them, <u>He that soweth</u>
> <u>the good seed is the Son of man</u>;
> 38 The field is the world<u>; **the**</u>
> **<u>good seed are the children of</u>**
> **<u>the kingdom</u>**; but the tares are
> the children of the wicked one;
> 39 The enemy that sowed them is
> the devil; the harvest is the
> end of the world; and the
> reapers are the angels. KJV

This takes us all the way back to the
Garden of Eden where Satan beguiled
(wholly seduced) Eve and she had
fraternal twins; Cain and Abel. Now we
are beginning to see why we have both
good and evil **seed,** children in the
world today.

> 1 John 3:9 Whosoever is born of
> God doth not commit sin; for his
> seed remaineth in him: and he
> cannot sin, because he is born of
> God. John 3:10-12 **In this the**
> **children of God are manifest, and**

the children of the devil:
whosoever doeth not righteousness
is not of God, neither he that
loveth not his brother.11 For
this is the message that ye heard
from the beginning, that we
should **Love One another.**

12 **Not as Cain, who was of that**
wicked one, and slew his
brother. And wherefore slew he
him? Because his own works were
evil, and his brother's
righteous. KJV

Side Note: Do you know why Cain Murdered
Abel?

Abel received the Father's blessings
because he listened to God and pleased
Him. Cain did not listen or cared less
about God's words. Cain was jealous of
his brother's blessings and after the
seeds of jealousy festered within him
they brought fourth fruit, Murder.

Why do you think the Terrorists want to
murder blessed Americans so bad? There
is nothing new under the sun.

The whole reason we are all here is to
plant seed (the true word of God) and in
so doing give everyone, whomsoever will,
an equal chance at salvation.

Now this is what the LORD says about
your Praise and worship songs along with
your burnt offerings. We will get to
what it is that the LORD wants from us
in a minute.

Amos 5:22-24 **Though ye offer me burnt offerings and your meat offerings, I will not accept them: neither will I regard the peace offerings of your fat beasts. 23 Take thou away from me the noise of thy songs; for I will not hear the melody of thy viols.** 24 But let **judgment** run down as waters, and **righteousness** as a mighty stream. KJV

Where do we learn judgment and righteousness?

Simply, these are found within the schoolmaster, Exodus, Lev. and Deut. This is a guide as to what is right and just. None of us are able to do that which is perfect or even good. For this reason Jesus came to save us from Satan, but mostly from our own destructive selves.

Let me explain. When we violate one of God's commands, it is like throwing a stone onto a smooth pond. It causes a ripple that goes all the way to the end. Call it God's law of the universe or whatever you like. Nevertheless, just like God's law of gravity. If you throw something up it will always come down. This is why Jesus came to take away the sins of the world.

You see, Jesus washed us in His blood (stops the ripple from turning into a tidal-wave that will return on our own heads) and brings us back into the place where our Father who is Holly and

Righteous will not see our filthiness. We can then enter into the Holy of Holies with Jesus and speak directly to our Father in the name of our mediator.

1 Tim 2:5 <u>For there is one God, and one mediator between God and men, the man Christ Jesus;</u> Heb 9:14-15 How much more shall the blood of Christ, who through the eternal Spirit offered himself without spot to God, purge your conscience from dead works to serve the living God? 15 <u>And for this cause he is the mediator of the new testament, that by means of death, for the redemption of the transgressions</u> that were under the first testament, they which are called might receive the promise of eternal inheritance. KJV

1 John 2:2-4 And he is the **propitiation** (Atonement) for our sins: and not for ours only, but also for the sins of the whole world. 3 And hereby we do know that we know him, if we keep his commandments. 4 <u>He that saith, I know him, and keepeth not his commandments, is a liar, and the truth is not in him.</u>

Propitiation: NT:2434 hilasmos (hil-as-mos'); atonement,

Our obligation is to understand how and why we have strayed from righteousness, repent (have a change of heart) try to do the right thing and humble ourselves before God asking forgiveness in Jesus' name who is faithful to forgive. If we are really sincere Jesus stops the ripple from reaching the end, returning back upon us and destroying us.

You see, our high priest, Jesus Christ stands at Yahveh's right hand and mediates the forgiveness of our transgressions before the Holy Father who then wipes the slate clean. Note: when Jesus was asked how many times should I forgive my brother if he repents (has a change of heart and really wants to do the right thing) He said,

> Luke 17:3-4 Take heed to yourselves: **If thy brother trespass against thee, rebuke him; and if he repent, forgive him**.
> 4 And if he trespass against thee seven times in a day, and seven times in a day turn again to thee, **saying, I repent;** thou shalt forgive him.

> Matt 18:22 Jesus saith unto him, I say not unto thee, Until seven times: but, Until seventy times seven.

> Heb 4:15-16 For we have not an high priest which cannot be touched with the feeling of our infirmities; but was in all points tempted like as we are, yet without sin.16 Let us therefore come boldly unto the throne of grace, that we may

obtain mercy, and find grace to
help in time of need. KJV

You see, Jesus, God with us wouldn't
command us to go through this flesh
without going through it   Himself also
with us. In my book that makes Him a
great leader; our High Priest
(mediator), King of Kings, and LORD of
LORD"S.
What a blessing. He knows all the
tribulations and temptations we are
going through. He understands and is
able to save our souls unto eternal
life.

Heb 5:5-6 So also Christ
glorified not himself to be made
an high priest; but he that said
unto him, Thou art my Son, to
day have I begotten thee. 6 As
he saith also in another place,
Thou art a priest for ever after
the order of Melchisedec.

Here is what the LORD says He wants from
us.

Hos 6:6 For I desired mercy, and
not sacrifice; and the knowledge
of God more than burnt
offerings. KJV

Mic 6:8
8 He hath shewed thee, O man,
what is good; and what doth the
LORD require of thee, but to do
justly, and to love mercy, and
to walk humbly with thy God?

225

Heb 10:11-13 And every priest standeth daily ministering and offering oftentimes the same sacrifices, which can never take away sins: 12 But this man, (Jesus Christ) after he had offered one sacrifice for sins for ever, sat down on the right hand of God;
13 From henceforth expecting till his enemies be made his footstool.
Heb 10:7-10 Then said I, **Lo, I come (in the volume of the book it is written of me,)** to do thy will, O God.

Here is the truth as Jesus spoke.

John 17:17 **Sanctify them through thy truth: thy word is truth.**

This is why Jesus kept warning us:

Matt 24:4 And Jesus answered and said unto them, Take heed that no man deceive you. Matt 24:5 For many shall come in my name, saying, I am Christ; (Christian) and shall deceive many. KJV

Do not let man or anyone else tell you that you need to give them your hard earned money in order for God to bless you. They are conning you, lying to you and ripping you off. Worst of all they are violating the third commandment, Exodus 20 -7 in using God's name in vain (emptiness) and in not following God's command to feed His sheep. You are to

226

give tithes to the priests, where you
are fed the word of God line by line and
verse by verse so that you may be armed
and able to stand in that evil day.

Matt 5:44-45 But I say unto you,
Love your enemies, bless them
that curse you, do good to them
that hate you, and pray for them
which despitefully use you, and
persecute you; 45 That ye may be
the children of your Father
which is in heaven: for he
maketh his sun to rise on the
evil and on the good, and
sendeth rain on the just and on
the unjust.

This means we are all God's children and
He loves all of His children.

This does not mean love someone who is
trying to kill you. That is stupid and
God is not stupid. This means love your
enemies who are God's enemies, who hate
even the mention of God's name. Reprove
them first and in doing so they may see
God in you and have a change of heart
and repent, then forgive them.

And so it shall be all the
way to the end.

Rev 12:17 And the dragon
was wroth with the woman,
and went to make war with
the remnant of her seed,
which keep the commandments
of God, and have the
testimony of Jesus Christ.
KJV

Chapter XX

Mystery Samaria.

What happened in Samaria in the past and how does this history relate to America, Europe, Canada, the free Christian Nations and Jerusalem today?

SAMARIA: see the sins of Samaria.

"History. Samaria was purchased from its owner, Shemer, for two talents of silver, by Omri, king of Israel, who "built on the hill, and named the city which he built Samaria, after the name of Shemer, the owner of the hill" (1 Kings 16:24). **From that time until the captivity of the ten tribes-about two hundred years-it continued to be the capital.**

During all this time **it was the seat of idolatry** (Isa 9:9; Jer 23:13; Ezek 16:46-55; Amos 6:1; Mic 1:1). There Ahab built a temple to Baal (1 Kings 16:32-33; cf. 2 Kings 10:35). On the other hand, it was the scene of the ministry of the prophets Elijah and Elisha (which see). Jehu broke down the temple of Baal but does not appear to have otherwise injured the city (10:18-28). The city was twice besieged by the Syrians, about 863 BC (1 Kings 20:1) and about 850 BC (2 Kings 6:24-7:20); but on both occasions the siege was ineffectual. **It was taken in 721 BC by Shalmaneser's successor, Sargon king of Assyria (18:9-10), and the kingdom of the <u>ten tribes</u> <u>was destroyed</u>.** In 331 it yielded to

Alexander the Great, who visited it on his way back from Egypt in order to punish the Samaritan murderers of the governor he had appointed over Coele-Syria. Ptolemy Lagos deemed it dangerous enough to have it dismantled before he gave over Coele-Syria to Antigonus; and, being rebuilt, it was again destroyed fifteen years later. It withstood a year's siege by John Hyrcanus, the Maccabee, before being taken by him. It was rebuilt by Gabinius, the successor of Pompey. Augustus gave Samaria to Herod, who fortified and embellished it and named it Sebaste, the Greek for Augustus. Herod built a Greco-Roman theater, a temple to Augustus, and a Roman-style forum and colonnaded road at the site.

In the NT it is recorded (Acts 8:5) that Philip "went down to the city of Samaria," which more literally means "into a city of the Samaritans." Still it is likely that the evangelist would resort to the capital city. Thus ends the Bible history of Samaria.

Archaeology. From 1908 to 1910 the site of Samaria was excavated by Harvard University under the direction of G. A. Reisner, D. G. Lyon, and C. S. Fisher (cf. Harvard Excavations at Samaria [1908-10], 2 vols. [1924]). From 1931 to 1933 excavation was continued by Harvard University, the Hebrew University of Jerusalem, the British Academy, the British School of Archaeology in Jerusalem, and the Palestine Exploration Fund under J. W. Crowfoot's direction. Further work was done in 1935 (cf. J. W.

Crowfoot, Kathleen M. Kenyon, and E. L. Sukenik, The Buildings at Samaria [1942]). These various excavations have revealed the following periods: (1) The Omri-Ahab Era, Periods I and II. (2) The Jehu Era, Period III. (3) The eighth century, when the city reached its acme of prosperity, Periods IV-VI. Stout walls from the Omri-Ahab Period and other fortifications reveal how Samaria could have held out against the Syrians (2 Kings 6:24-30) and against the powerful Assyrians (17:5). Large numbers of cisterns were also discovered, compensating for the lack of natural water supply. **The famous Samarian ostraca are usually placed in the reign of Jeroboam II in the eighth century. These inscribed pieces of pottery were recovered in one of the palace** storehouses. They are accounts of royal revenue received in the form of oil and wine. Numerous stewards are mentioned, recalling biblical names such as Nimshi, Ahinoam, and Gomar (Gomer). Also numerous ivories in the form of plaques or furniture inlays were recovered. Portrayed on the ivories are papyrus reeds, lotus, lions, bulls, sphinxes, and Egyptian gods such as Isis and Horus. The high artistic quality and the Egyptian gods indicate strong foreign influence at this period. **These ivories recall the "beds of ivory" and "houses of ivory" denounced by Amos (Amos 3:15; 6:4; cf. 1 Kings 22:39).** Some of the significant remains at the site today include the palace of Omri and Ahab, the temple to Augustus, the Greco-Roman theater, a gate complex with Hellenistic towers, a basilica adjacent to the

forum, and part of the colonnaded
street."
(from The New Unger's Bible Dictionary.
Originally published by Moody Press of
Chicago, Illinois. Copyright (c) 1988.)

What is the sin of Samaria and who is
being referred to?

> Micah: Mic 1:1-2 The word of
> the LORD that came to Micah
> the Morasthite in the days of
> Jotham, Ahaz, and Hezekiah,
> kings of Judah, which he saw
> concerning Samaria and
> Jerusalem.

> 2 Hear, all ye people;
> hearken, O earth, and all
> that therein is: and let the
> Lord GOD be witness against
> you, the Lord from his holy
> temple.

> Mic 1:5 **For the transgression
> of Jacob is all this, and for
> the sins of the house of
> Israel.** What is the
> transgression of Jacob? is it
> not Samaria? and what are the
> high places of Judah? are
> they not Jerusalem?

If you have read the chapter about
America in the Bible you should know who
Israel is that is being spoken to. Is it
not like Samaria?

> Mic 1:5-7 **For the
> transgression of Jacob
> (natural seed line of the**

house of Israel) is all this,
and for the sins of the house
of Israel. What is the
transgression (H-6586
rebellion and falling away)
of Jacob? is it not Samaria?
and what are the high places
of Judah? are they not
Jerusalem?

6 Therefore I will make
Samaria as an heap of the
field, and as plantings of a
vineyard: and I will pour
down the stones thereof into
the valley, and I will
discover the foundations
thereof.

7 And all the graven images
thereof shall be beaten to
pieces, and all the hires
thereof shall be burned with
the fire, and all the idols
thereof will I lay desolate:
for she gathered it of the
hire of an harlot, and they
shall return to the hire of an harlot.
KJV

So you don't think we worship idols here
in America?

Here is what the king knows will happen
if the people learn their heritage and
return again to the LORD.

1 Kings 12:26 And Jeroboam
said in his heart, Now shall
the kingdom return to the
house of David:

1 Kings 12:27-31 **If this people go up to do sacrifice in the house of the LORD at Jerusalem, then shall the heart of this people turn again unto their lord,** even unto Rehoboam king of Judah, and **they shall kill me,** and go again to Rehoboam king of Judah.

The King knows that when the people learn the truth about their heritage, who they are and return to the LORD, the people will kill him and throw out the unjust judges, priests and leaders. So the King sets up a diversion, deception, conspiracy or what ever you call it to draw the people away from the truth whereby he can hold them captive to him and his system.

28 Whereupon the king took counsel, and **made two calves of gold,** and said unto them, It is too much for you to go up to Jerusalem: **behold thy gods, O Israel,** which brought thee up out of the land of Egypt.

This is a lie. God by Moses brought the children out of Egypt. Those who followed the golden calf set up in the wilderness perished. We are either really stupid or no one reads our History.

29 And he set the one in Bethel (house of God), and

the other put he in Dan.

30 And **this thing became a
sin**: for the people went to
worship before the one, even
unto Dan.

The king set up his own priests in all
the churches that were directed by him
to weaken the people and further his
conspiracy.

These priests were not Levites, ordained
of God.

31 And **he made an house of
high places, and made priests
of the lowest of the people,
which were not of the sons of
Levi**.

1 Kings 12:32-33 And Jeroboam
ordained a feast in the
eighth month, on the
fifteenth day of the month,
like unto the feast that is
in Judah, and he offered upon
the altar. So did he in
Bethel, sacrificing unto the
calves that he had made: and
he placed in Bethel the
priests of the high places
which he had made.

33 So he offered upon the
altar which he had made in
Bethel the fifteenth day of
the eighth month, even in the
month which he had devised of
his own heart; and ordained a
feast unto the children of

Israel: and he offered upon
the altar, and burnt incense.

**None of these feasts are written as and
ordinance by God for His children to
follow. Another step in weakening the
children by substituting something false
for the truth.**

2 Kings 13:6 Nevertheless
they departed not from the
sins of the house of
Jeroboam, who made Israel
sin, but walked therein: and
there remained **the grove** also
in Samaria.) KJV

Grove: OT:842'asheyrah (ash-ay-raw');
from OT:833; happy; Asherah (or Astarte)
a Phoenician goddess; also an image of
the same:

Happy Easter, we're going to be Raptured
out of here at any moment. Remember the
chapter about what went on around the
Asherah pole?

Another example of the false traditions
set up.

Ezek 13:2-14:1 Son of man,
prophesy against the
prophets of Israel that
prophesy, and **say thou unto
them that prophesy out of
their own hearts,** Hear ye
the word of the LORD;
3 Thus saith the Lord GOD;
**Woe unto the foolish
prophets, that follow their
own spirit, and have seen**

nothing!

OH! I see a man with a arthritis problem and he is being healed out there in TV land right now. Let's see, out of 300,000 people out there, what are the odds that someone thinks they have arthritis? What are the odds that one of those people will not really have arthritis but think they did and it is gone? IT'S A MIRACLE!!!

> 4 **O Israel, thy prophets are like the foxes in the deserts.**
> 5 **Ye have not gone up into the gaps, <u>neither made up the hedge for the house of Israel to stand in the battle in the day of the LORD</u>.**

Are they teaching you the battle plan and how to be armed and protected in that day?

> 6 <u>**They have seen vanity = emptyness and lying divination, saying, The LORD saith: and the LORD hath not sent them:**</u> and they have made others to hope that they would confirm the word.

> 7 <u>Have ye not seen a vain vision, and have ye not spoken a lying divination,</u> <u>**whereas ye say, The LORD saith it; albeit I have not spoken?**</u>

8 Therefore thus saith the Lord GOD; Because ye have spoken vanity, and seen lies, therefore, behold, I am against you, saith the Lord GOD.

9 And mine hand shall be upon the prophets that see vanity, and that divine lies: they shall not be in the assembly of my people, neither shall they be written in the writing of the house of Israel, neither shall they enter into the land of Israel; and ye shall know that I am the Lord GOD.

Peace Peace (Jer: 8 11) and there was no peace. Don't worry about the tribulation, you're going to be gone.

10 **Because, even because they have seduced my people, saying, Peace; and there was no peace;** and one built up a wall, and, lo, others daubed it with untempered morter:= whitewa.11 **say unto them which daub it with untempered morter, that it shall fall:** there shall be an overflowing shower; and ye, O great hailstones, shall fall; and a stormy wind shall rend it.

12 Lo, **when the wall is fallen, shall it not be said unto you, Where is the**

daubing wherewith ye have
daubed it?

The false Christ is here. Why are you
still here? You were supposed to be
gone?

13 Therefore thus saith the
Lord GOD; I will even rend
it with a stormy wind in my
fury; and there shall be an
overflowing shower in mine
anger, and great hailstones
in my fury to consume it.
14 **So will I break down the
wall that ye have daubed
with untempered morter, and
bring it down to the ground,
so that the foundation
thereof shall be discovered,
and it shall fall, and ye
shall be consumed in the
midst thereof: and ye shall
know that I am the LORD.**

15 Thus will I accomplish my
wrath upon the wall, and
upon them that have daubed
it with untempered morter,
and will say unto you, The
wall is no more, neither
they that daubed it;16 **To
wit, the prophets of Israel
which prophesy concerning
Jerusalem, and which see
visions of peace for her,
and there is no peace, saith
the Lord GOD.**

17 Likewise, thou son of man, **set thy face against the daughters of thy people, which prophesy out of their own heart;** and prophesy thou against them,

18 And say, Thus saith the Lord GOD; <u>Woe to the women that sew pillows to all armholes, and make kerchiefs upon the head of every stature to hunt souls! Will ye hunt the souls of my people, and will ye save the souls alive that come unto you?</u>

You ever so gentle prophets, preachers and teachers that cover over God's outstretched saving arms with your traditions and lies.

19 <u>And will ye pollute me among my people for handfuls of barley=$$ and for pieces of bread, to slay the souls that should not die, and to save the souls alive that should not live, by your lying to my people that hear your lies?</u>

20 <u>Wherefore thus saith the Lord GOD; Behold, I am against your pillows, wherewith ye there hunt the souls to make them fly, and I will tear them from your arms, and will let the souls go, even the souls that ye</u>

<u>hunt to make them fly.</u>

Hunt the souls to make them fly, hum!!

God's outstretched arms covered over with pillows. Whitewashed their own walls of lies with flying out of here teachings instead of the true word of the LORD.

21 Your kerchiefs also will I tear, and deliver my people out of your hand, and they shall be no more in your hand to be hunted; and **ye shall know that I am the LORD.**

22 Because with lies ye have made the heart of the righteous sad, whom I have not made sad; and strengthened the hands of the wicked, that he should not return from his wicked way, by promising him life: 23 Therefore ye shall see no more vanity, nor divine divinations: for <u>**I will deliver my people out of your hand: and ye shall know that I am the LORD.**</u> KJV

We have seen that the sin of Samaria is the worshiping of false gods, traditions that make void the word of God, and corruption along with conspiracy.

What is this conspiracy?

The conspiracy is to keep the Heritage, History and truth from the people lest they return to the Lord and bring that which is; righteousness, justice, truth and Holiness back into the land and the Lord takes pity and repents of His anger.

> Matt 25:31-32 When the Son of man shall come in his glory, and all the holy angels with him, then shall he sit upon the throne of his glory:
>
> 32 <u>And before him shall be gathered all nations:</u> and <u>he shall separate them one from another, as a shepherd divideth his sheep</u> from the goats:
> KJV

Those who are raptured need not attend. They forgot the meaning of the word all Nations.

Acknowledgements

I would like to thank Pastor Arnold Murray and Pastor Lancelot Knight for their unwavering dedication to teaching God's Word as it is written with particular attention to rightly dividing the word and their dedication to the TRUTH as the warning is being sent fourth.

If you want to learn something it is wise to go to the source first and then look for an educated teacher who is dedicated to the languages, history and truth as properly seen in God's words and always check them out yourself with the proper tools.

For more in-depth study and understanding please see.

Pastor Arnold Murray of Shepherds Chapel. http://www.shepherdschapel.com/
P.O. Box 416 Gravette, AR 72736
1-800-643-4645
Send for free tape. Mark of the Beast.

Lancelot Knight of Kings Chapel.
http://www.kingschapel.org/
P.O. Box 791 Hershey, PA 17033
1-888-746-9827
Send for free booklet. The Plan of God.

Strong's Exhaustive Concordance for Greek, Hebrew and Aramaic translations. By James Strong, LL.D., S.T.D.

ISBN 1-41205312-9